Crowning Clinton

WHY HILLARY SHOULDN'T BE IN THE WHITE HOUSE

CROWNING CLINTON
WHY HILLARY SHOULDN'T
BE IN THE WHITE HOUSE

Compiled and Edited by Victor Thorn

ISBN: 978-0-9881997-9-8

Published by:
AMERICAN FREE PRESS
16000 Trade Zone Avenue, Unit 406
Upper Marlboro, MD 20774-8789

Ordering more copies:

Order more copies of *CROWNING CLINTON* (softcover, 118 pages, $12 plus $4 S&H) from AMERICAN FREE PRESS, 16000 Trade Zone Avenue, Unit 406, Upper Marlboro, MD 20774. Call 1-888-699-6397 toll free to charge copies to Visa, MasterCard, AmEx or Discover. See more products online at www.AmericanFreePress.net.

Subscriptions to AMERICAN FREE PRESS newspaper:

A subscription to AMERICAN FREE PRESS newspaper is $49 for one year (26 bi-weekly issues) and $89 for two years (52 biweekly issues) inside the U.S. Outside the U.S. prices vary. You can also order at www.AmericanFreePress.net. See a special subscription offer at the back of this volume or call toll free number above and ask for best current subscription offer.

Reproduction Policy:

Material in this publication may be reproduced without prior permission in critical reviews and other papers if credit is given to author, full book title is listed and full contact information and subscription information are given for publisher as shown above.

WHY HILLARY SHOULDN'T BE
IN THE WHITE HOUSE

VICTOR THORN

PUBLISHED BY AMERICAN FREE PRESS

DEDICATION

This book is dedicated to Juanita Broaddrick, Eileen Wellstone, Elizabeth Ward Gracen, Regina Hopper Blakely, Bobbie Ann Williams, Kathleen Willey, Lencola Sullivan, Sandra Allen James, Susie Whitacre, Kathy Bradshaw, Cristy Zercher, Paula Jones, Monica Lewinsky, Gennifer Flowers, Dolly Kyle Browning, Sally Perdue, Betty Dalton, Denise Reeder, and scores of other women across America that were raped, sexually assaulted, molested, or improperly compromised by Bill Clinton. All of these victims were either attacked by Hillary Clinton and her henchmen, or their crimes were mocked, marginalized, and dismissed by this so-called bastion of "feminism."

TABLE OF CONTENTS

SECTION THREE: Twisted Predators

SECTION FOUR: Money

SECTION FIVE: Foreign Policy

Scandals

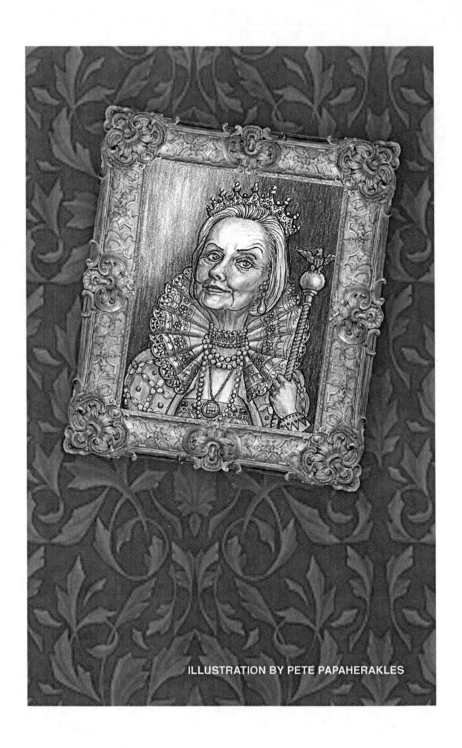

ILLUSTRATION BY PETE PAPAHERAKLES

The Preponderance of Evidence Against Hillary Clinton

T here's an old saying that carries a great deal of truth: "A nation deserves the politicians that it elects." In light of this cautionary phrase, the most pertinent question each of us must ask is: does America deserve Hillary Clinton as its president? From my perspective, the resounding answer is emphatically "No."

With my *Hillary (and Bill)* trilogy serving as a foundation, the book you are about to read continues the sordid Clinton tale of political subterfuge, illicit sex, greed, massive foreign policy failures, and endless scandals. Some of these articles were previously published in the pages of AMERICAN FREE PRESS (AFP), while others have never before appeared in print. Either way, AFP continually outshines its counterparts in the corporate mainstream media, especially since most of them don't possess the courage to even touch this damning material at all.

This news doesn't bode well for Bill and Hillary Clinton,

who remain prototypical insiders and the most powerful couple in Washington, D.C. history. In addition to being first lady in both Arkansas and the Oval Office, Mrs. Clinton's resume includes two terms as a New York senator, four years as secretary of state, a Bilderberg attendee (as was her husband Bill), plus memberships in the highly influential Council on Foreign Relations (CFR) and Trilateral Commission (TC). She has also run for president twice.

Moreover, Hillary acted as a clandestine Central Intelligence Agency (CIA) asset used to infiltrate antiwar movement groups at Yale University, as well as serving on the Watergate committee that investigated President Richard M. Nixon.

Prior to her arrival in the nation's capital, Hillary rose to prominence at the Rose Law Firm, while also working behind the scenes as a key figure in the Mena drug trafficking crime enterprise.

Last but not least, Hillary is largely recognized as the primary architect of 1993's mass murder siege at Waco in which 76 Branch Davidians were killed (including 21 children), while also being implicated in the political hits and cover-ups of Vince Foster, Commerce Secretary Ron Brown, among others.

Anyone that has read Hillary (and Bill): The Sex, Drugs and Murder volumes, realizes that there exists no line whatsoever which these psychopaths won't cross. For years, longtime Spotlight and AFP icon Michael Collins Piper referred to this trilogy as the hands-down gold standard of exposés ever written about the Clintons. Others agree.

In early 2016, Polish publisher Wektory will release a translated version of this three-book series in Poland.

An even greater tribute arose when bestselling authors

Roger Stone and Robert Morrow included this dedication in their 2015 book, *The Clintons' War on Women*:

> Dedicated to the women and men violated by Bill and Hillary Clinton in their scramble for power. And also to Sean Hannity, Nick Bryant, Matt Drudge, Peter Schweitzer, Daniel Halper, Michael Goodwin, Christopher Hitchens, David Sirota, Paul Sperry, Ed Klein, Brent Scher, Victor Thorn, Marinka Peschmann, Ambrose Evans-Pritchard, Jim Nelson, Roger Morris, Sally Denton, and Chris Ruddy. These journalists have done more than anyone else to expose the Clintons' epic transgressions.

To be mentioned among these researchers and media personalities is quite an honor. At any rate, considering the amount of material that I've compiled over the years on the Clintons, presenting a compendium of arguments as to why Hillary and Bill should never again reenter the White House would be easier than picking low-hanging fruit from an apple tree. For example, Bill Clinton's 1993 promotion of the Community Reinvestment Act directly led to the 2007-2008 housing crash. Or, during her tenure at the State Department, Hillary's neocon tendencies led to bloodbaths in Libya and across the Middle East. Even more recently, as a government employee, she illegally maintained a private email server to conceal how the Clinton Foundation acted as a vast multi-million dollar private slush fund. They used a similar *modus operandi* while co-governors during the 1980s. At that time, Bill and Hillary created the Arkansas Development Finance Authority as a means of laundering money that their partners in crime then kicked-back as campaign donations. If the Clintons find a methodology that allows them to get away with their dirty dealings, they use it over and over.

Obviously, on another note, sex and hypocrisy have forever played an integral role in the Clintons' marriage and public lives. During an April 23, 2015 AFP radio interview conducted by AFP Web Editor Dave Gahary, I stated:

> Hillary doesn't like women. She pretends to be a champion of women's causes, but she doesn't like them. If she did, she wouldn't allow her serial sexual predator rapist husband Bill to keep getting away with what he's done for the last three or four decades. Nobody covers up for his activities and acts as a handler more than Hillary Clinton does. There are a string of women who say that Bill raped, sexually molested, or fondled them.

As a means of intimidation, Hillary repeatedly entered the picture and used her 'nuts and sluts' attack tactics. Imagine, Hillary is supposedly the greatest champion of women's rights since Eleanor Roosevelt (her hero), yet that's what she brazenly called the women who had been victimized and severely traumatized by her husband. It goes without saying that she targeted these women because they jeopardized the Clintons' future as rising stars on the political scene.

I continued in this interview, "Hillary sees women as competition and as the things that her husband preys upon when he's committed adultery thousands and thousands of times."

During this same interview, Gahary commented that a member of the U.S. Secret Service's Presidential Protective Detail once confided to him that they'd caught Hillary in sexually compromising positions with other women in the White House. I replied, "When Bill was having his prolonged affair with Gennifer Flowers in Arkansas, she once asked him if Hillary was a lesbian. Bill told her, 'Hillary has [had sex with more women] in her lifetime than I have.' This comment came straight from her husband." Coincidentally, I once spoke with Gennifer Flowers for nearly two hours via telephone, and she confirmed that this exchange occurred between her and Bill.

In 2011, legendary Bilderberg hound Jim Tucker penned an AFP article entitled "Senate OKs Sodomy for GIs" in which he lamented Hillary's subversive leanings. "Mrs. Clinton delivered an impassioned speech on behalf of homosexuals, bisexuals, lesbians, and transgender people at the Human Rights Council in Geneva on December 6, 2011," Tucker sneered.

To nearly every one of these accusations, Hillary would respond that she's being victimized by some sort of hidden, furtive cabal. In fact, Michael Collins Piper addressed this topic in his anthology *Dirty Secrets: Crime, Conspiracy, and Cover-up During the 20th Century* by chronicling how Hillary propounded the theory that a vast "right-wing conspiracy" was intent on destroying her husband, especially in regard to his adulterous affair with intern Monica Lewinsky. However, in terms of strategically placed media leaks that unmasked his White House dalliances with Lewinsky, Piper dropped this bombshell. "Could it have been someone in Al Gore's camp—close to the White House—eager to move the Vice President into the Oval Office? That's speculation, of course, but not beyond the realm of possibility." Indeed, the Clintons have not garnered a great deal of loyalty over the course of their careers, especially when you consider how many people they've stepped over and discarded to reach their desired goals.

Speaking of which, when I interviewed author, radio talk show host, publisher, and Power of Prophecy founder Texe Marrs in 2011, he proposed, "Monica Lewinsky was a Jewish Mata Hari spy of the Mossad placed in the White House by Rahm Israel Emanuel. Then, a few years ago, [Bill] Clinton reportedly had an affair with Lisa Belzberg [who was married to Matthew Bronfman]. The Bronfmans were upset about this tryst, which could explain why Hillary—who is half-Jewish on her mother's side—lost to Obama in 2008. Bill Clinton couldn't make it up to them, even when declaring during a speech that if Israel was ever attacked, he'd fight and die for them on the front lines."

Jim Traficant, an iconoclastic nine-term Ohio Congressman, once wrote along these same lines for AFP. "If you recall, the President Clinton-Monica Lewinsky soap opera broke open in one day. President Clinton's advisors told him to deny everything. He did. Suddenly, President Clinton's body fluids ended up on one of Monica's secretly kept dresses and the whole soft-porn drama came roaring into history. I said, and was quoted often in many media sources, 'If it's on the dress, he must confess.' At some point, President Clinton finally admitted to oral sex."

The Clintons' three-ring circus extends well beyond carnal shenanigans. For instance, during a 2015 AFP interview, presidential candidate Merlin Miller explained to this writer how, as secretary of state, Hillary's infamous pushing of the "reset" button with Russia in 2009 has led to the worst relations between our nation and theirs since the Cold War. Rather than uniting with Russia, Mrs. Clinton's actions were those of a saboteur.

With virtually no accomplishments or legitimate successes during her stint as Barack Hussein Obama's secretary of state, Hillary instead created immense amounts of global havoc that the world is still suffering through today. AFP correspondent Pete Papaherakles highlighted Clinton's callousness in a 2011 article. "After news reports declared Libyan leader Muammar Qadaffi dead, Secretary of State Hillary Clinton could not hide her blatantly bloodthirsty giddiness as she boasted about the cold-blooded murder. 'We came, we saw, he died,' she exclaimed. Considering the "Clinton Body Count," she's quite familiar with the subject of having blood on one's hands. Although Qadaffi's convoy put up white flags of surrender, a tradition respected in warfare since the days of the Roman Empire, North Atlantic Treaty Organization (NATO) drones bombed it to smithereens anyway. They then proceeded to brutally torture, sodomize, and murder the country's leader of 42 years. His son was also killed, as was his daughter and three grandchildren years ago. Hillary had much to cheer about."

Hillary's heartlessness also became apparent during an interview conducted by AFP Web Editor Dave Gahary with retired CIA intelligence analyst Ray McGovern. Gahary explained:

> McGovern remained standing about 12 yards away from Hillary Clinton [at a February 15, 2011 speech given at George Washington University]. He

next removed his jacket to reveal a Veterans for Peace t-shirt, and then turned his back to the secretary in silent protest. . . . McGovern explained in an exclusive interview with AFP, "I was standing there motionless, speechless, not saying a word. All Clinton could see on the back of my shirt was Veterans for Peace. Then, without warning, I was literally blindsided, hammer-locked to the head and dragged out into the aisle. I could see Hillary speaking during this episode, and she didn't miss a syllable." McGovern continued, "I wasn't heckling. I didn't say a word. I stood there with my back to the secretary not making a motion or a word, silently, when I was set upon by two goons, lifted bodily above the four women who were sitting between me and the aisle, and dragged out of the place before I could figure out what was happening to me."

Inexcusably, Mrs. Clinton didn't halt these strong-arm bullying tactics or try to protect Mr. McGovern in the least. Nor did she object that his First Amendment rights were being grossly violated.

Scores of further illustrations could be provided, but at this juncture, let's return to page one of this introduction, whereupon I asked, "Does America deserve Hillary Clinton as its president?" After completing the contents of this book, it seems incomprehensible that any sane-minded reader could respond in the affirmative.

—VICTOR THORN
Happy Valley, Pa.
January 1, 2016

Stop Hillary

HILLARY'S TIES TO SAUL ALINSKY EXPOSED

Do Americans want another president who's the disciple of a Jewish socialist named Saul Alinsky? Interestingly, during the 2008 Democratic primaries, both candidates, Barack Hussein Obama and Hillary Diane Rodham Clinton, were acolytes of the radically extreme Alinsky. This situation is reminiscent of the 2004 presidential election where two Skull and Bonesmen, George W. Bush and John F. Kerry, vied for the White House.

The Alinsky problem reemerged again with the recent disclosure of adoring letters sent by Hillary to Alinsky in 1971. In this correspondence, she told Alinsky that she "missed their regular conversations" and thanked him for his advice on campus activism. Regrettably, her ties to this man extend much deeper than mere communiques. Not only did she write her undergraduate thesis on Alinsky, she also met with him several times, invited him to speak at Wellesley College, and nearly came under his employ.

Who precisely is Saul Alinsky? According to Mark Davis and Emmett Tyrrell in the book *Madame Hillary*, he's responsible for writing "the left-winger's operating manual for revolution" in his landmark tome, *Rules for Radicals: A Pragmatic Primer for Realistic Radicals*. Incidentally, as an indication of his character, Alinsky dedicated this subversive how-to book of guerilla tactics to Lucifer. In regard to his philosophy, Alinsky advocated a combination of political relativism and situational ethics. In *Rules for Radicals*, he pronounced, "The end justifies almost any means." Alinsky also boasted, "Ethical standards must be elastic," and, "All effective actions require the passport of morality."

Relying on techniques such as agitation, conflict and friction, Alinsky realized that "hope and change," a phrase he proudly inspired, wouldn't result from burning the system down, but by infiltrating it. Commonly known as the father of community organizing, Alinsky's overt shakedown policies of Chicago businesses were later adopted by race-hustler Jesse Jackson.

Speaking of the Windy City, in his 1996 biography, David Brock referred to Chicago native Hillary Clinton as "Alinsky's daughter." Similarly, Obama worked for Alinsky organizations in Chicago, taught seminars on his methods as a professor, and adopted this man's stratagems of class warfare. After all, Alinsky urged, "The organizer's first job is to create issues or problems."

These disturbing connections take on an even more ominous tone. In a January 13, 2008 article entitled "Hillary, Obama and the Cult of Alinsky," Richard Poe made some startling revelations. In addition to Alinsky learning many of his gutter intimidation ploys from Al Capone's top enforcer, a gangster named Frank Nitti, he was also highly promoted by Jewish Wall Street tycoon Eugene Meyer. It should be noted that Meyer served as Federal Reserve chairman during the 1930s and owned *The Washington Post*, an unabashed Bilderberg mouthpiece.

To get more insights on this sordid rabble-rouser, on September 23 this writer interviewed Peter Schramm, a Senior Fellow at the Constitutionally-based Ashbrook Institute. When asked why Hillary's letters to Alinsky are important, Schramm replied, "People need to be reminded of her left-wing past that fell right in line with Alinsky's radicalism of the 1960s. Hillary went along with all of Alinsky's calls for social revolution, and it's disingenuous of her to now hide it."

Schramm provided more historical context. "Alinsky led a transformation of '60s radicals that included Trotskyite and Leninist cells. Their first targets weren't Republicans, but ordinary liberals who defended the Constitution. Alinsky's New Left attacked old-fashioned Democrats because they weren't radical enough. Although it took them awhile, Barack Obama is the first example of an Alinskyite New Left president."

Coinciding with Obama's coronation at the 2008 Democratic National Convention, L. David Alinsky, Saul's son, told *The Boston Globe* on August 31, 2008, "I'm proud to see that my father's model for organizing is being applied successfully beyond local community organizing to affect the Democratic campaign in 2008."

Considering Obama's vow to "fundamentally transform America," it doesn't seem particularly odd that when Hillary Clinton reached out to Alinsky in 1971, she was employed in ultra-liberal Berkeley, California at the leftist law firm Treuhaft, Walker and Bernstein. Some of their primary clients were Black Panthers and other violent militants.

Hillary's boss of Jewish descent, Robert Treuhaft, served

as the Communist Party USA's official attorney. In *Hell to Pay*, author Barbara Olson stated, "[Treuhaft] dedicated his entire legal career to advancing the agenda of the Soviet Communist Party and KGB."

Following this stint, Clinton next landed a prime spot on the House Judiciary Committee's Watergate investigative team in 1974. How did she get this job? Conveniently, another Jewish Alinsky devotee, Marian Wright Edelman, used her influence to open doors for Hillary.

Utilizing a deadly ruthlessness to obtain her political objectives, Davis and Tyrrell offered these words of wisdom on Hillary Clinton's first rule of politics. "In the struggle for power, tactics take precedence over principles." Apples don't fall far from their trees, and not surprisingly, in *Rules for Radicals*, Alinsky determined, "The end is what you want, and the means is how you get it."

After two terms of Obama's scandal-ridden train wreck in the White House, it's clear that America cannot survive four more years with another one of Alinsky's sycophants occupying that seat.

SAY IT AIN'T SO: BUSH OR CLINTON IN 2016?

For years the real possibility of another Bush and Clinton facing off in the 2016 presidential election caused a collective groan of apprehension across many parts of America. One political activist voicing his disapproval is Nelson Hultberg, director of Americans for a Free Republic and president of the Dallas, Texas-based National Independent Party.

During a January 7, 2015 interview, Hultberg told this writer, "Jeb Bush running against Hillary Clinton would be a total disaster because it epitomizes what people are against, specifically a Democrat/Republican monopoly. Bush and Clinton are both big government statists. We don't have two political parties any longer. As Pat Buchanan remarked, 'They're two wings of the same bird of prey.' Democrats and Republicans are taking us down the road of tyranny."

When asked what it represented if someone entered a polling booth and pulled the lever for either Bush or Clinton, Hultberg responded, "They're defending the status quo of these two parties. Democrats that support Clinton symbolize the pathetic nature of modern-day politics. Hillary is pitiful. She's a socialist ideologue that's leading a march toward doom for America. Democrats will destroy themselves if they nominate Hillary."

In regard to the potential GOP nominee, Hultberg commented, "Jeb Bush equals Hillary-light. Plus, let's not forget that George Herbert Walker Bush and Bill Clinton conspired together behind-the-scenes during the Iran-Contra scandal. Of course they did. These two families are interchangeable. They're the face of America's power structure."

This same reasoning applies to Congress, as Hultberg noted. "Leaders like John Boehner, Nancy Pelosi, Mitch McConnell and Harry Reid control all newly elected incoming legislators. It doesn't take long for these politicians to realize who butters their bread. They either get bought off or come under their hammer."

The recent opposition to House Speaker Boehner by conservative Republicans is a perfect example, especially the blowback directed against them for not toeing the line. Hultberg surmised, "Boehner and Pelosi teach their subordinates who and what to vote for. They've been placed in these positions of power so that everyone else follows along. If this structure remains, we'll never break the Democrat-Republican monopoly."

If a Bush or Clinton does enter the White House following the 2016 election, Hultberg envisions disastrous results. "I see a bleak future of business as usual. The Demopublicans will continue their Keynesian economic plan where they keep creating more and more debt to sustain growth. Under this inflationary spiral, I predict a huge economic crash. Because both establishment parties preach globalism and want Keynesian fiat money, they'll further push us toward world government and a world bank."

Still, Hultberg feels that hope remains if a viable third party candidate can emerge. "Forty to 50% of Americans don't believe in the malarkey happening in Washington, D.C. We must appeal to those whose eyes are still open. Lord Acton said, 'Power tends to corrupt, and absolute power corrupts absolutely.' The Republicans and Democrats have no competition. Considering this state of affairs, Victor Hugo once stated, 'Nothing is more powerful in history than an idea whose time has come.' In the past, voters weren't ready for an independent candidate, but now they are."

POLITICAL STRATEGIST RUES HILLARY PRESIDENCY

Clinton horror stories extend back decades: Whitewater, Mena drug trafficking, the murders of Vince Foster and Ron Brown, plus the concealment of violent sex crimes against women such as Juanita Broaddrick. More recently, the Benghazi cover-up leads undeviatingly to Hillary's doorstep.

With millions in a campaign war-chest, Mrs. Clinton elicits comparisons to either a queen ready for coronation or corrupt Chicago mobsters like Al Capone.

Needless to say, a variety of groups have already formed with one specific goal in mind: to ensure that Hillary never becomes president. One of these organizations, the Stop Hillary Political Action Committee (PAC), has issued the following admonition. "Today there is no more powerful, well-connected politician in America who threatens to do real harm to the American way of life than Hillary Clinton."

On January 31, 2015 this writer interviewed Garrett Marquis, spokesman for the Stop Hillary PAC. When questioned about the potential dangers of another Clinton in the White House, Marquis replied, "History shows why we need to be wary of her. When it comes to scandals, whether ethical or legal, Hillary's been either directly accused or an accomplice in so many of them. She's a political opportunist, and has been her entire life."

In terms of Hillary's cozy, hypocritical relationship with Wall Street and the financial industry, Marquis, pointed out, "It's not surprising that she criticizes big banks one day and then receives $400,000 the next from Goldman Sachs. Hillary is a liberal elitist, and has been ever since hustling her way into the White House."

Marquis added, "We need to remember how Bill and Hillary sold the Lincoln bedroom [in the White House] to the highest bidder. She continues to sell herself out to whoever donates the most money. The PACs that support her have already collected millions of dollars."

Echoing the nefarious "Clinton Body Count," Marquis next addressed recent revelations about how Hillary's aides compiled a numerical enemies list of Democrats that sup-

ported Barack Obama instead of her in 2008. Topping this
list was current Secretary of State John Kerry, who the Clintons categorized as "treacherous." "It's clear," Marquis said,
"that if anybody crosses her, Hillary wages a vendetta against
them. I don't want someone as president who writes down
names of enemies and then takes them out."

When mention of how Obama officials unleashed Inter-
nal Revenue Service (IRS) officials on their political foes,
Marquis remarked, "Hillary and Bill are even worse. They
epitomize dirty politics. They've never worried about skirting
ethical or moral boundaries to get what they want. They'll
keep using these same practices to deceive the American
public about their actual goals."

Going beyond mere rhetoric, the Stop Hillary PAC filed
a lawsuit against Hillary. Marquis explained, "A super PAC
named "Ready for Hillary" rented Clinton's 2008 email list,
which is a direct violation of FEC (Federal Election Commission) laws. We intend to hold them accountable." (The lawsuit was rejected on an FEC technicality.)

On a closing note, Marquis issued another insightful ob-
servation. "Barack Obama and Hillary Clinton are linked
through their policies, the liberal infrastructure, donors, and
their ties to George Soros. But I have no doubt that when
Hillary announces her candidacy, she'll not only run against
the GOP, but also Obama's failures as a president, many of
which she was part of."

THE CLINTON-OBAMA WARS

For decades, every time a new controversy enveloped her,
Hillary blamed it on a "vast right wing conspiracy." But, are

high-ranking officials within the Obama White House actually the ones attempting to sabotage her 2016 presidential bid? Many factors indicate that a long-standing power struggle between the Obamas and Clintons is now surfacing via strategically placed leaks, media innuendo, and downright ad hominem attacks.

On September 10, 2015 this writer interviewed Ann Ubelis, a radio talk show host and member of South Carolina's Beaufort Tea Party. Ubelis stated, "I've spoken to secret service agents from both camps, and they say there's definitely bad blood. From what I understand, Obama's top advisor, Valerie Jarrett, known as the Black Widow, is feeding information to the press. Or, she's having others in the White House do it for her. It's all orchestrated and controlled."

The circumstances that initiated this feud are quite compelling, as Ubelis noted. "It was widely reported that during the 2008 Democratic primaries, Bill Clinton told Massachusetts Senator Teddy Kennedy, 'A few years ago, this guy [Obama] would have been carrying our bags.'"

Ubelis continued, "Right now, there's a battle going on for who'll take control of the Democratic Party. Obama and Jarrett want to extend their political influence into the future. My big question is: what qualifications does Jarrett have to be Obama's top advisor other than being a slumlord from Chicago?"

In his bestselling book *Blood Feud: The Clintons vs. the Obamas,* author Ed Klein says that not only do these two factions despise each other, but that Jarrett and Michelle Obama privately refer to Mrs. Clinton as "Hildebeast." In addition, after Obama's hatchet men smeared Bill Clinton as a racist during the 2008 primaries, according to Klein the former president sneered, "I hate that man Obama more than any man I've ever met, more than any man that ever lived."

Also, numerous sources point to Jarrett as the main driving force behind revelations that Mrs. Clinton used a private email server during her tenure as secretary of state. This scandal involves a variety of prickly aspects, from the illegality and security risks of placing top secret data in jeopardy to Hillary's influence peddling for the Clinton Foundation. She is now being investigated by the Federal Bureau of Investigation (FBI).

As AFP has reported for nearly three years, Hillary spearheaded an off-the-books weapons running operation in Libya that funneled guns, ammunition and other armaments to anti-Assad forces in Syria. When the U.S. consulate got attacked on September 11, 2012, resulting in the deaths of four Americans, it caused a considerable amount of embarrassment for the Obama administration.

Jarrett, acting as Obama's cloak-and-dagger Machiavelli, never forgave Mrs. Clinton, nor was she ever comfortable with her appointment as secretary of state. Klein revealed that once at a meeting inside the Oval Office, discussions became so heated that Hillary actually became physical, jabbing Obama in the chest with a finger to highlight her argument.

Editor Mac Slavo went so far as to intimate in a March 17, 2015 column on his website SHTFplan.com: "The President and Valerie Jarrett are prepared to eat their own, and [they'll] stop at nothing to keep Hillary out of the White House."

Benghazi

THE BENGHAZI TIMELINE EXPOSED

On the 11th anniversary of September 11, when four Americans were slain in Benghazi, a Predator drone equipped with cameras hovered over a safe house that was under attack and beamed images—via satellite in real-time—to the State Department, Pentagon and CIA headquarters in Langley. Also, during an October 11, 2012 radio interview with Howie Carr of Boston's WRKO, Colonel David Hunt stated that over 100 people watched this feed in the White House Situation Room.

All of these entities witnessed firsthand that the onslaught did not result from protests over an anti-Mohammed video. The "fog of war" didn't blur what they saw, as Hillary Clinton asserted, nor were the details sketchy, as administration officials claimed. Moreover, the State Department's Charlene Lamb admitted during Congressional hearings that they watched the attacks in real-time.

To reinforce that this assault did not arise from a "spontaneous uprising," at 4:05 p.m. EST on September 11,

Hillary's State Department Operations Center issued an urgent email alert. "Approximately 20 armed people fired shots. Explosions have been heard as well." At no time did they mention protests or a video. Two hours later, at 6:07 p.m., the State Department transmitted another email. "Ansar al Sharia claims responsibility for Benghazi attack."

The blame placed on Ansar al Sharia—a group the U.S. government says is affiliated with al-Qaeda—did not emanate from the Mossad, Dick Cheney, or *The Weekly Standard*. Rather, it came directly from the Obama administration's State Department. In this light, every party involved knew with certainty from day one that the attacks did not arise from some type of protest. In 2015 when Hillary's use of a private email server was uncovered, investigators learned that she told her daughter Chelsea on the evening of the Benghazi attacks that al-Qaeda type terrorists had committed these atrocities, yet then blatantly lied to the American public and the families of slain victims by blaming it on a YouTube video.

At any rate, for the next two weeks following this carnage, Barack Obama and his cronies outwardly lied about the circumstances surrounding this attack against American personnel. Beginning with a September 12 Rose Garden statement, Obama generically referred to "acts of terror," but never called the murders "terrorists." However, on that same day, Libya's deputy ambassador to London stated that Ansar al Sharia was behind the attacks, while on September 13 Libya's ambassador to the U.S. specifically referred to the ambush as terrorism.

Below is a damning timeline of deception which emanated from the Obama administration:

Sept 14: White House Press Secretary Jay Carney said, "We don't have and did not have concrete evidence to suggest that this was not in reaction to the film."

* * *

September 16: U.S. Ambassador to the UN Susan Rice appeared on five Sunday talk shows to say, "In fact, it was a spontaneous—not a premeditated—response to what transpired in Cairo." [i.e., reaction to the video]

* * *

September 18: Jay Carney reiterated, "Our initial information, and that includes all information, we saw no evidence to back up claims by others that this was a preplanned or premeditated attack. We saw evidence that it was sparked by a reaction to this video."

* * *

September 18: Obama said to David Letterman, "Terrorists used [film protests] as an excuse to attack."

* * *

September 19: Jay Carney, as questions surfaced about the attackers carrying shoulder-launched rocket-propelled grenades, said, "We have no evidence of a preplanned or premeditated attack."

* * *

September 20: Obama during an interview with Mexico's *Univision* that took place in Miami, said, "What we do know is that the natural protests arose because outrage over the video was used as an excuse by extremists."

* * *

September 24: When asked while appearing on *The View* if the Benghazi attacks were terrorism, Obama referred to them as a "mob action."

* * *

September 25: During his UN speech, Obama was still beating a dead horse, citing the anti-Mohammed video six separate times.

A PREMEDITATED TERRORIST ATTACK

In an October 18, 2012 analysis of the Benghazi attacks, former CIA Clandestine Operations Officer Claire Lopez wrote, "They let our ambassador and others die, in real time, watching it happen, and they didn't do anything about it." Elaborating further, Lopez stated that after U.S. Navy SEALs were told to stand down three separate times, such an order not to assist fellow Americans had to reach, at a minimum, Hillary at the State Department, or higher.

At a time when every American embassy should have been on high alert—especially since Ambassador Stevens had repeatedly requested additional security for months— how could a CIA safe house be attacked for hours on end without a response from the most powerful military on earth? Incredibly, two of the four murdered Americans were killed seven hours after the attacks began. It should be noted that Israel's assault on the USS *Liberty* lasted for two hours. Such amateurish incompetence on the part of this administration is difficult to fathom.

As evidence undeniably shows, the attacks were premeditated and well planned. Spontaneous mobs supposedly angered by a YouTube video don't carry rocket-propelled grenades, mortars, machine guns and AK-47 rifles. After attackers doused the mission with diesel fuel and set it on fire, Stevens ultimately died of smoke inhalation in a safe-room. His bodyguard Sean Smith burst through a window, only to be killed moments later by a volley of grenades.

These men undoubtedly knew their lives were in danger, as Stevens frantically issued emails to the Pentagon warning of increased violence. Months earlier he pleaded with the State Department about being on a hit list. "What we have seen are not random crimes of opportunity, but rather targeted discriminate attacks." Indeed, their Benghazi compound had been bombed twice prior to September 11. Likewise, shortly before his death, Navy SEAL Sean Smith posted a message on a gaming site, "I hope we get out alive."

Tragically, as the White House, CIA and Pentagon watched the attacks as they unfolded, Barack Obama met with Defense Secretary Leon Panetta at 5:00 p.m. No rescue troops were sent to directly assist these Americans, and later—as the carnage continued—Obama went to bed. The next day he callously flew to Las Vegas and attended a fundraiser.

NO SYMPATHY FOR VICTIMS' FAMILIES

On October 11, 2012 Pat Smith, mother of Sean Smith who was slain in Benghazi on September 11, told CNN's Anderson Cooper about the reaction she received at his September 19 funeral. "I look at TV and see bloody handprints on walls thinking, my God, is that my son's? They [the Obama administration] haven't told me anything. They're still studying it, and the things they are telling me are outright lies. Susan Rice talked to me personally and said, 'This is the way it is, it was because of this film that came out.'"

On top of Ms. Rice's unmitigated duplicity, Mrs. Smith described our commander-in-chief as unsympathetic beyond words. "I cried on Obama's shoulder, and then he looked off into the distance, so that was worthless to me."

Racked with grief, she relayed more of her encounter. "I said [to Obama]: You screwed up. You didn't do a good job. I lost my son, and he said: We'll get back to you; trust me. Well, I don't trust you anymore."

On October 24, Charles Woods, father of slaughtered Navy SEAL Tyrone Woods, spoke with conservative radio talk show host Lars Larson about his encounter with Obama at the funeral. "When he came over to our little area, he kind of mumbled, 'I'm sorry.' His face was looking at me, but his eyes were looking over my shoulder like he couldn't look me in the eye. It wasn't a sincere, 'I'm really sorry that your son died,' but it was more of an insincere, whining 'I'm sorry,' and it was like shaking hands with a dead fish. It just didn't feel right. Now it's coming out that, apparently, the White House Situation Room was watching our people die in real time."

Likewise, he explained the secretary of state's cold-heartedness. "[Hillary] came over separately and talked. I gave her a hug, and she did not appear to be one bit sincere at all."

Lastly, during an October 26 televised interview, Woods said of the president. "Was [Obama] one of those cowards in the White House watching my son being murdered on TV and refusing to do anything? That's a question he probably won't have the courage to answer publicly."

BENGHAZI: THE STILL HIDDEN STORY

Finally, after two months, the mainstream media began to at least partially touch upon the Benghazi attack's covert aspects. As reporters Adam Entous, Siobhan Gorman and Margaret Coker of *The Wall Street Journal* admitted on November 1, 2012, "The U.S. effort in Benghazi was at its heart a CIA operation."

Shortly after the Obama administration's commencement of a NATO-led invasion of Libya where Muammar Qadaffi was eventually murdered, the CIA established their first intelligence annex in February 2011. With Hillary's State Department providing diplomatic cover to conceal this operation's true nature, CIA contractors recruited anti-Qadaffi rebels, provided weaponry to them, and then tracked shoulder-fired missiles ransacked from the Libyan military following the government's collapse.

Most importantly, strong evidence exists that slain CIA ambassador Chris Stevens commandeered the transfer of these seized weapons from Libya, through Turkey, into Syria where CIA-Mossad created rebels are battling President Bashar Assad's army.

According to a September 14 article by *The Times* of London, "A Libyan ship carrying the largest consignment of weapons for Syria since the uprising began has docked in Turkey and most of its cargo is making its way to rebels on the front lines."

"Among more than 400 tonnes of cargo the vessel was carrying," wrote *The Times*, "were SAM-7 surface-to-air anti-aircraft missiles and rocket-propelled grenades (RPGs), which Syrian sources said could be a game-changer for the rebels.

On November 9, 2012 this writer interviewed a source that requested to be used only as "background" for this story. When asked if he felt that forces who originally worked with the CIA and NATO to overthrow Qadaffi attacked the CIA safe house because they were angered that their bounty— thousands of high-tech weapons—were now being taken from them and dispatched to another group of CIA mercenaries in Syria, the source stated, "The Libyans were pawns in their own revolution. NATO and the Obama administration wanted Qadaffi out, so they used the home team to do it. Soldiers that opposed Qadaffi received their funding from NATO and the CIA. Then, after these rebels did the dirty work and got rid of Qadaffi, the CIA went searching for his heat-seeking missiles."

Once the CIA planted roots in Libya, this individual picked up the story of what transpired: "Some of the same forces that were set against Qadaffi were later used to provide security at the CIA's safe house. Although many of the details are still clouded, it's certain that the CIA embassy was not attacked due to an anti-Islamic film, as the administration initially claimed."

When this writer inquired as to whether President Obama would have been apprised and directly knowledgeable of the CIA's weapons-running operation, he responded with one-word succinctness: "Yes."

To illustrate how extensively the CIA had its fingers in this entire mess, the source continued, "Of the 30 men stationed in Benghazi, only seven weren't officially employed by the CIA. Then, once the mission was attacked, CIA contractors got most of their fellow Americans out. Yet, following their rescue mission, they were tracked down and ultimately killed."

In regard to the blowback which resulted from this disastrous operation, the source stated, "For at least 30 days prior to the September 11 onslaught, Ambassador Stevens' emails prove that he felt an attack was imminent. But since the CIA had already moved a majority of weapons out of Libya on the September 6 boat dispatched to Turkey, there was no more need for the mission in Benghazi. Now that most everyone knows about this situation, the CIA's cover was blown, which is something they never wanted."

Lastly, this writer inquired as to whether there was any possibility that Stevens had been deliberately set-up. "At the very least, somebody was negligent about security at the embassy, and Stevens knew more about the Libyan gun-running operation than anyone."

Now, conveniently, almost according to script, Stevens is dead and CIA Director David Petraeus resigned on November 9 due to "marital indiscretions." As of this writing, he won't testify on Capitol Hill about his role in the Benghazi scandal unless subpoenaed.

HILLARY'S HIDDEN HAND: WEAPONS TRAFFICKING

The dirty secret is simple: Benghazi's Special Mission Compound served as the hub for a CIA program to arm rebels battling against Syrian President Bashar al-Assad. According to an April 29, 2013 column by political commentator Katie Kieffer, "Obama, former Secretary of State Hillary Clinton and then-CIA Director David Petraeus were likely behind [this] gun-trafficking program."

To launch this updated version of Iran-Contra, in August

2011 Clinton proposed the plan to Petraeus, who assigned U.S. Ambassador Christopher Stevens to handle the secret logistics.

Stevens's importance proved crucial. Earlier, in March 2011, military experts largely cite him as the man in charge of deposing Libyan strongman Muammar Qadaffi. Following this mission, Stevens next relocated to Benghazi, where he began amassing an arsenal of at least 20,000 shoulder-launched missiles, RPGs, and infrared honing surface-to-air devices.

To facilitate arms shipments to Syria, Stevens worked with a man named Abdelhakim Belhadj of the Libyan Islamic Fighting Group. By November 2011, Belhadj was meeting with Free Syrian Army leaders to arrange the deals.

To secure a crucial 40,000 ton shipment of armaments, on September 2, 2012 Petraeus met with Turkish PM Erdogan in order for his country to act as a conduit into Syria. Four days later a Libyan vessel named *Al Entisar* arrived in Iskenderun, Turkey carrying this explosive cargo.

On May 9, 2013 *Liberty News* revealed details about the point man for these transactions. "Stevens had dealt with applications coming from U.S. weapons dealers requesting licenses to sell arms to Libyan insurgents." Finally, on September 11, 2012 Stevens negotiated in Benghazi with two CIA cutout organizations before his final meeting with Turkish Consulate General Ali Sait Akin. On Aug 1, 2013 award-winning journalist Jim Hoft of the conservative website *Gateway Pundit* summarized what transpired. "Turkey was the staging ground through which Syrian-bound guns and rebels were smuggled . . . Mr. Akin and Co. made a substantial financial contribution [to Stevens] and left."

WHO ORDERED THE STAND-DOWN IN BENGHAZI?

With four U.S. personnel killed and at least seven wounded during an eight-hour attack, why weren't military forces dispatched to the Benghazi consulate and annex?

On August 5 and 8, 2013 this writer spoke with David Smith, cofounder of the blog "Barracuda Brigade." To set the tone for these interviews, Smith stated, "According to our military sources, I can say with 98% certainty that the Benghazi attacks were uplinked by overhead drones to networks that included the White House Situation Room, State Department and CIA headquarters so they could monitor the attacks in real-time. Yet almost immediately, Barack Obama issued a stand-down order before watching people die on camera. He then got up the next morning for a campaign rally in Las Vegas."

When questioned about the possibility of a full-scale rescue, Smith answered, "We've categorically confirmed that the U.S. military had ships in Libyan waters 20 minutes away. It would have taken 10 minutes prep time and 10 minutes flight time, but Obama issued a stand-down order."

Expanding on this notion, Smith continued, "There's only one office with the authority to prevent a military response, and that's the president's. Commanders in the field were prepared to respond, and later as a result, two of them were court-martialed while another was removed from duty."

Providing more details, Smith explained, "A diplomatic security agent named David Ubben, along with two former Navy SEALs, rejected the stand-down orders so they could defend our men. During a rooftop firefight, Ubben—profusely bleeding—fired laser markers with GPS coordinates so that any ships or jet fighters within range could intervene. These guys on the ground fully expected help to arrive, but none ever came. Ubben still lies in Walter Reed Hospital today."

As to the motivation behind this executive decision, Smith offered a theory. "Being seven weeks before the 2012 election, Obama had no intention of retaliating against the responsible parties at Benghazi. The reason why is that since weapons were being delivered to al-Qaeda rebels in Syria, it's an act of treason to aid, arm and abet a known enemy. It's a violation of both federal and international law. Obama wasn't going to respond against the attackers, so he tried to let details about his administration's arms-trafficking die there."

Smith provided a closing thought. "Both entrenched political parties have their hands dirtied in this affair. As for Obama, since U.S. personnel were attacked, why is no one with information allowed to talk? It's like telling a rape victim she can't testify against her assailant. How is it constitutionally acceptable for a president to remove an individual's right to speak by silencing them?"

LIBYAN PATSY TAKES THE FALL

Veteran researchers familiar with the concept of political patsies immediately smelled a rat when, on August 6, 2013 U.S. prosecutors announced that they'd filed a sealed criminal complaint against a Libyan man named Ahmed Abu Khattalah. However, similar to Lee Harvey Oswald's infamous response that he hadn't been charged with killing JFK, the Department of Justice (DoJ) refused to specify any of the accusations brought against Khattalah.

Why then, after nearly a year, did the DoJ and FBI finally

decide to pursue Khattalah, especially since Fox News, the UK's *Daily Mail*, the AP, and *The Huffington Post* interviewed or identified Khattalah last October? The answer, quite simply, is that the White House had been shamed into it after CNN's Arwa Damon spoke with Khattalah at a hotel coffee shop in Benghazi only days earlier.

As Representative Jason Chaffetz (R-Utah) told reporters, "CNN was able to talk to one of the suspected terrorists. How come the FBI isn't doing this and CNN is?"

Who, precisely, is this supposed ringleader? As the admitted leader of a de facto al-Qaeda terror group called Ansar al-Sharia, Khattalah had been arrested and imprisoned in Libya by Muammar Qadaffi's security police for posing a threat to his regime.

Upon his February 2011 release, Khattalah eventually migrated to Benghazi, where he confessed to being present at the September 11, 2012 attacks. He dismissed, though, any role in orchestrating or participating in the melee.

His plea rings true, particularly because he's been a suspect since day one yet has never been questioned by the feds. Speaking freely, Khattalah told Reuters last October, "Here I am in the open, sitting at a hotel with you." Similarly, he informed Damon that, despite scores of FBI agents in Benghazi, "The investigative team did not try to contact me."

15 DEAD WITNESSES IN BENGHAZI

On January 15, 2014 a bipartisan Democratic-led Senate Intelligence Committee revealed that since the September 11, 2012 terrorist attacks against a U.S. consulate in Benghazi where four Americans were killed, 15 Libyan witnesses who were cooperating with FBI investigators have been murdered.

Along with a House Armed Services Committee report released days earlier, both panels issued searing condemnations while arriving at definitive conclusions. First, General Carter Ham, head of the U.S. Africa Command (AFRICOM), testified in June 2013 that, almost immediately, he informed Defense Secretary Panetta and Joint Chiefs of Staff Chairman Martin Dempsey that a terrorist attack was in full-swing.

In addition to footage obtained from onsite CCTV cameras, Panetta and Dempsey then met with Obama at the White House. All of these individuals knew that the carnage didn't result from an anti-Muslim video. Still, by September 25, 2012—a full two weeks later—Obama continued his deceptive fantasy narrative during an appearance on *The View* by claiming he wasn't sure what happened.

These dual reports also contained some other explosive conclusions: (a) the attacks were completely preventable, (b) four specific al-Qaeda affiliated terrorist groups, including a former GTMO detainee, orchestrated the onslaught, (c) Hillary Clinton's State Department received at least seven reports prior to September 11 warning of imminent dangers, (d) the White House still refuses to provide witnesses and documents to investigators, and (e) to this day not one person within the Obama administration has been held accountable.

As expected, neither report referenced the biggest bombshell of all. Namely, that overwhelming proof exists that seized Libyan weapons were being channeled from Benghazi to anti-Assad rebels in Syria.

To present a broader perspective on the matter of 15 potential witnesses being eliminated, this writer interviewed three leading researchers. First, on January 16, 2014 this

SECTION TWO: BENGHAZI | 41

writer contacted Dean Garrison, editor of the online news site "D.C. Clothesline."

Garrison stated, "The reports are that these witnesses were killed, which tells me they were murdered. You don't have to look far to find a long list of convenient deaths related to both Hillary Clinton and Barack Obama. My gut feeling is that some or all of these people were silenced so that they wouldn't cooperate with the FBI."

On January 17, 2014 Tim Brown, founder of the conservative-based website "Freedom Outpost" shared a similar view. "We have to face a reality. When we talk about corruption in Washington, D.C., people like Hillary Clinton are willing to off people. Witnesses in Benghazi are dying in spades. Those in charge of this cover-up are leaving a trail of bodies in their wake. Is this the kind of people we want leading us?"

Lastly, *Washington Times* columnist and radio talk show host Sara Marie Brenner offered this perspective. "In terms of the 15 dead witnesses, it appears that the Obama administration is getting rid of anyone that knew the full story in the weeks leading up to this attack in Benghazi."

Brenner added, "This information should shock us, but unfortunately it doesn't. With the president and his regime, if you speak out against them, you're placed on a list. They can't take a chance that the whole Benghazi affair will blow up in their faces. So, now we have 15 dead Libyans. If you're not in the Obama camp, they'll do whatever it takes to intimidate you."

BENGHAZI SCANDAL REVISITED

As one of the first publications in America to reveal how the real Benghazi story involved illegal weapons-trafficking (and not a ridiculous YouTube video), AFP continues its mission to reveal what other news sources conceal, just as we've done with the USS *Liberty* assault, OKC bombing, and 9-11.

On September 12, 2012—one day after the Benghazi attacks—Barack Obama appeared in the White House Rose Garden and pledged to capture those responsible for this onslaught. Nearly a year later, not a single assailant has been arrested, and no charges were filed until August 6, 2013. Amid a slew of bald-faced lies and ongoing cover-ups, Obama and his spokesmen now refer to Benghazi as a "phony scandal."

But if Benghazi were merely a fake brouhaha, why are CIA officials subjecting key personnel to monthly lie detector tests and bullying them into silence? Secrecy and intimidation at the "Company" is so unprecedented that it's been compared to the Manhattan Project.

In order to quiet those present at Benghazi, an unnamed insider told CNN on August 1, 2013 what his colleagues are being forced to endure. "It is pure intimidation . . . you have no idea the amount of pressure being brought to bear on anyone with knowledge of this operation." If pertinent details were divulged, he fretted, "You don't [just] jeopardize yourself. You jeopardize your family as well."

To date, Obama seems asleep at the wheel on this issue, similar to September 11, 2012 when he retired to bed early instead of providing military aid for endangered personnel. Today, rather than mocking genuine investigators, shouldn't Obama officials be providing details on the identities of at least 20 survivors?

On August 2, 2013 Representative Trey Gowdy (R-S.C.) accused the Obama administration of changing names, creating aliases, and shifting personnel to undisclosed locales around the country. "What creates the appearance and perhaps the reality of a cover-up?" Gowdy asked. "Not letting us [speak] to the people who have the most amount of information."

Senator Rand Paul (R-Ky.) voiced the same concerns on May 9, 2013. "I'm a little curious when employees of the State Department are told by government officials they shouldn't testify before Senate or House committees, and then they're sequestered."

Speaking of the State Department, a finger of blame must also be directed at former secretary of state Hillary Clinton. During January 23, 2013 testimony before the Senate Foreign Relations Committee, Paul directly questioned Hillary about weapons trafficking from Libya to Turkey. Clinton feigned ignorance, replying, "Nobody's ever raised that with me."

As a fixer extraordinaire for her entire political career, Hillary seemed to be working hand-in-hand with CIA spooks to scrub the Benghazi annex of any evidence. On August 1, 2013 Dr. Mark Christian, the Egyptian-born founder of Global Faith Institute—a website specializing in Middle Eastern history—revealed, "While Secretary of State Hillary Clinton was ignoring the body of American Ambassador Christopher Stevens, she was ordering that all of Stevens' classified information in Tripoli be destroyed."

On October 5, 2012 Susan Posel, chief editor of the website "Occupy Corporatism" wrote, "The crime scene in Benghazi was left to be destroyed by CIA-operatives dressed up as rioters to contaminate the evidence."

Although Posel's claims are unverifiable, on May 9, 2013 *Liberty News* confirmed part of her story: "The CIA immediately jumped into action, scrubbing the annex facility of any trace of CIA operations. All documents, files, traces of a clandestine presence were completely removed and/or destroyed." Could this erasure of evidence explain why the Benghazi CIA compound was left unguarded for three weeks and not inspected by FBI investigators?

THE BENGHAZI-BEACON GLOBAL CONNECTION

It's a scandal bigger than Watergate, the October Surprise and Iran-Contra, yet the breadth of this illegal weapons trafficking operation involving high-ranking government officials linked to a military-industrial outfit named Beacon Global Strategies (BGS) may prevent the actual truth from ever emerging. Instead, dog-and-pony congressional committees continue to divert attention by focusing on talking points, emails and videos. (BGS, formed in 2013, has become the updated version of the post 9-11 Carlyle Group.)

AFP was one of the first media outlets to report on the primary players at the heart of this matter: "In August 2011 secretary of state Hillary Clinton proposed the [smuggling of armaments from Libya to Syria] to CIA Director David Petraeus, who assigned U.S. Ambassador Christopher Stevens to handle the logistics of this clandestine operation."

This information was verified by two sources. Famed investigative journalist Seymour Hersh confirmed that the CIA's Petraeus and Clinton's State Department oversaw the "black operations." Secondly, on April 22, 2014 the Citizens Commission on Benghazi cited former CIA agent Clare Lopez, who revealed that the intelligence community and State Department briefed top leaders in Congress on this unlawful enterprise.

Meanwhile, in early 2012, the Obama administration arranged financing from Qatar and Saudi Arabia for the Libyan-Syria transport, with Turkish President Recep Erdogan acting as their pivot-man.

Proof of these extra-governmental rat-lines arrived when the CIA's number two man under Petraeus, Mike Morell, testified on April 2 before a House Intelligence Committee that 33 CIA agents were on the ground in Benghazi when the attacks occurred. However, analysts at Langley quashed their reports of what transpired in favor of a more watered-down version, none of which mentioned arms sales. Morell is currently a counselor at BGS and Hillary Clinton consultant.

Moreover, in a January 15, 2014 Senate Intel report, General Carter Ham, head of AFRICOM, stated, "[I] was not even aware there was a CIA annex in Benghazi." He also divulged that Stevens twice refused Department of Defense (DoD) security offers. General Ham also testified that his primary contact in Benghazi was Andrew Shapiro, former assistant secretary of state under Hillary Clinton and BGS cofounder.

When news of the Benghazi onslaught surfaced, on-the-ground Benghazi station chiefs realized within 15 minutes that a terrorist attack was transpiring, not a protest fueled by a YouTube video. They immediately informed General Ham, who next notified Defense Secretary Panetta at the White House. Interestingly, Panetta's chief of staff at that time was Jeremy Bash, another BGS cofounder.

In turn, Panetta met with President Obama in the Oval Office to update him on this tragedy. As panic spread through the White House, the State Department's Hillary Clinton prepared step one of the cover up. Namely, she issued the following statement at 10 p.m. on September 11. "Some have sought to justify this vicious behavior as a response to inflammatory material (i.e., video) posted on the Internet."

Let there be no doubt: Hillary initiated the anti-Muslim video red herring. By her side in constructing this smoke-screen was senior advisor Philippe Reines, who's been de-scribed as Clinton's principal gatekeeper and fixer. Reines was also another BGS cofounder.

The importance of subverting the truth in regard to their gun-running scheme by blaming it on a video that only aired in Egypt for a few minutes on September 9, 2012 surfaced when Judicial Watch obtained a previously concealed email originating from Obama's deputy national security advisor Ben Rhodes. On May 1, 2014 Judicial Watch's director of pub-lic affairs Jill Farrell told this writer, "These documents were provided in response to a court-ordered FOIA lawsuit. They contained narrowly defined information behind the talking points that former UN Ambassador Susan Rice used on the September 16, 2012 Sunday morning talk shows." Coinciden-tally, Ben Rhodes' brother, David, is the president of CBS News, the same organization that hired Mike Morell of BGS.

Bringing this sordid mess full circle, specifically the amount of effort exerted on concealing criminal activities, for-mer Bill Clinton senior advisor Dick Morris announced in April, 2014, "Congressman Mike Rogers (R-Mich.), as Chair-man of the House Intelligence Committee, was charged with investigating the adequacy of security at the Benghazi com-pound prior to the September 11, 2012 attack. His wife, Kristi Clemens Rogers, was president and CEO of the company [AEGIS Defense Services] contracted by [Hillary Clinton's] State Department to provide that security."

Who, pray tell, was Mike Rogers' staff director: none other

than Michael Allen, another BGS cofounder.

In all, we see a pattern of plausible deniability at the CIA, State Department, and inside the White House. By establishing a pattern of fall guys—intel analysts at Langley, Susan Rice, and bureaucrats in the West Wing—Petraeus, Clinton and Obama have been successful at leading a compliant media and compromised legislators on numerous wild goose chases. Regrettably, the latest "smoking gun" emails relating to how talking points were edited stands as little more than another tactic to divert public attention away from the Obama administration's sordid history of weapons-trafficking that includes Fast and Furious, Libya, Syria, and now the Ukraine.

BENGHAZI COVER-UP & INTIMIDATION CONTINUES

The most recent assault on whistleblowers revolves around the Obama administration's attempts to silence individuals whose accounts of the September 11, 2012 Benghazi consulate attack differ from the official version.

Attorney Victoria Toensing, who represents Greg Hicks, Deputy Chief of Mission at the U.S. Embassy in Libya, stated on April 30, 2013, "People have been threatened, and not just at the State Department. People have been threatened at the CIA . . . It's frightening, and they're taking career people and making them well aware that their careers will be over."

A special operations member, speaking on condition of anonymity, told reporter Adam Housley on April 30, 2013 that, in direct contradiction to the White House account, military troops had enough time to intervene on September 11 and save those who were eventually slain. Yet, instead of responding, they were instructed to stand down and abandon their countrymen.

This whistleblower told Housley, "You've got guys in the Special Ops community who are still active and involved, and they would be decapitated if they came forward with information that could affect high-level commanders."

The explosive details being concealed by Obama and his inner circle extend far beyond lies about the Benghazi slaying as, allegedly, a spontaneous uprising triggered by an anti-Islamic video.

On April 29, 2013 columnist and political commentator Katie Kieffer confirmed what AFP reported months ago. "President Obama, former Secretary of State Hillary Clinton and then-CIA Director David Petraeus were likely behind a mishandled gun-trafficking program that ended up arming radical jihadist rebels who stormed the U.S. consulate and CIA annex in Benghazi."

Kieffer went on to describe how weaponry seized after the U.S.-NATO-led Libyan invasion was funneled through Turkey to anti-Assad forces fighting in Syria. In addition, other arms such as machine guns and rocket-propelled grenades were sold directly to Qatar, Saudi Arabia and Turkey.

LIES SHOULD DISQUALIFY HILLARY AS PRESIDENT

How many more lies must Hillary Clinton get caught making before her supporters accept that, even by Washington, D.C. standards, she's too corrupt to be president? On December 9, 2015, Judicial Watch received verifiable proof that shortly after the September 11, 2012 Benghazi attacks had begun, a high-ranking Pentagon official notified Hillary's State Department in an attempt to save American personnel whose lives were in danger that fateful night.

At 7:19 p.m. ET, Department of Defense Chief of Staff Jeremy Bash urgently reached out to three of Hillary's top aides—Jacob Sullivan, Wendy Sherman, and Thomas Nides— informing them that the Pentagon had assets in place and were ready to intervene in the unfolding attacks that ultimately lasted for nearly eight hours. All they required was Hillary's approval. Tragically for the men who lost their lives during subsequent attacks, Hillary never responded to the DoD request.

This de facto stand-down order is seen by many pundits as a smoking gun. First, not only did the Obama administration conceal Bash's email for over three years, but both Hillary and DoD Secretary Panetta testified under oath that (a) no military forces were available that evening, and (b) they could not have reached the Benghazi compound in a timely fashion while it was under siege.

But Bash unequivocally stated, "After consulting with General Dempsey, General Ham, and the Joint Staff, we have identified the forces that could move to Benghazi." More importantly, since the Benghazi attacks began at 3:40 p.m. ET, and Bash sent his email at 7:19 p.m. ET, the onslaught continued for another four hours until nearly midnight.

Hillary and Panetta lied, and, in doing so, Americans lost their lives. Gregory Hicks, deputy chief of mission at the U.S. Embassy in Tripoli, testified before Congress on May 8, 2013: "If we had been able to scramble a fighter or aircraft over Benghazi as quickly as possible after the attack commenced, I believe there would not have been a mortar attack on the annex because I believe the Libyans would have split. They would have been scared to death that we would have gotten a laser on them and killed them."

Why did Hillary and her co-conspirators order this stand-down and sacrifice lives? Quite simply, they didn't want to draw any attention to their illegal CIA-State Department weapons trafficking operation that transported guns and heavy artillery from Libya to Syria. If exposed, those behind these crimes would have been guilty of violating the Geneva Conventions, multiple international laws, and the United Nations (UN)'s Arms Trade Treaty.

On August 1, 2013, CNN's Drew Griffin and Kathleen Johnston verified the seriousness of these offenses: "The CIA is going to great lengths to make sure whatever it was doing remains a secret."

Even earlier, an October 5, 2012 Defense Intelligence Agency (DIA) report determined: "Weapons from the former Libya military stockpiles located in Benghazi were shipped to the ports of Banias and Borj Islam, Syria." U.S. intelligence agencies and the State Department were clearly aware of these lethal weapons shipments.

One final bit of proof arose during a May 11, 2015 interview conducted by Fox News anchor Brett Baier. He asked former CIA Deputy Director Mike Morell, "Were CIA officers tracking the movement of weapons from Libya to Syria?"

Morell responded, "I can't talk about that," and then shifted the blame, making a veiled reference to the utilization of cutout groups.

"Whether we were watching other people do it [trafficking weapons], I can't talk about it," he said.

Twisted Predators

BILL CLINTON TIED TO THE D.C. MADAM?

H as another name been added to the long list of government-sponsored murders, with possible chief suspects belonging to the Bush-Clinton crime cabal?

The body of 52-year-old "D.C. Madam," Deborah Jeane Palfrey, was found in a shed near her mother's Sun Valley mobile home in Tarpon Springs, Florida on the morning of May 1, 2008. Although Captain Jeffrey P. Young revealed that at least two apparent suicide notes were discovered, suspicions are running high that foul play was involved in her hanging via a nylon rope. For starters, less than 10% of all female suicides are attributed to hanging—a statistical rarity—and according to journalist Mick Gregory, "In the United States, hanging is the least "popular" way to off yourself . . . Of all female suicides, very few are by hanging. It's been out of fashion for the past 100 years."

There are plenty of other clues that Palfrey was murdered, but prior to delving into them, an overview of what was at stake should first be provided to understand how threatening this woman was to the Beltway power brokers. On April

15, 2008 Palfrey was convicted by a federal jury of racket-
eering, money laundering, illegally using the U.S. mail, and
running an upscale $250/hour prostitution ring in Washing-
ton, D.C.—all of which fell under the government's Racket-
eer Influenced and Corrupt Organizations Act, RICO,
statutes. Potentially facing four to six years in prison, her
maximum imprisonment could have stretched to 55 years,
yet that was unlikely. Sentencing was scheduled for July 24.

What propelled this story into the national headlines was
a client list of up to15,000 names that included Washington's
political and business elite, including high-ranking National
Aeronautics and Space Administration members, officials from
the International Monetary Fund and World Bank, corporate
CEOs, White House and Pentagon employees, and lobbyists.

Palfrey's "little black book" of telephone numbers
weighed 46 pounds and had already caused the resignations
of Republican Senator David Vitter of Louisiana, as well as
Randall L. Tobias, Deputy Secretary of State to Condoleezza
Rice. Others specifically named in these phone logs were dis-
graced toe-sucker and advisor to Bill Clinton, Dick Morris,
along with Harlan K. Ullman, a military strategist who came
up with the "shock and awe" strategy used for America's
Iraqi Invasion in 2003.

What most worried Washington's political elite was Ms.
Palfrey's defiant attitude. As reported by Paul Duggan in *The
Washington Post*, on April 16, 2008, "Palfrey announced that
she would make public some of her records, exposing ex-
clients from the more refined walks of life in the nation's
capital." In another interview, she threatened, "I can state
with unequivocal certainty this situation will be a very long
and unpleasant one. I'm sure as heck not going to federal

prison because I'm shy about bringing in the deputy secretary of whatever." Palfrey also let it be known that she would be willing to sell her little black book, and it was rumored in publishing circles that a book deal was about to be signed.

The stakes got even higher when Palfrey's attorney, Montgomery Blair Sibley, said in 2007 that even though a firm price had not yet been established for this book, "If Bill Clinton's on the list, that's a different matter than somebody nobody's ever heard of before."

Was Sibly simply dropping names, or did he know something more? Some researchers have linked Clinton's name to a September 1994 batch of phone records originating from Washington's Park Hyatt Hotel, yet corroborating evidence is not strong enough at this time to prove these assertions to be factual. Still, when we consider information presented in *Hillary (and Bill): The Sex Volume*, we learn that Clinton's consigliere, Bruce Lindsey, used to scurry Clinton to the Marriott Hotel in downtown D.C. for extramarital affairs—a distance of little more than one mile from the Park Hyatt. In light of the former president's sexual proclivities, it's not hard to imagine that he used multiple locales for his trysts.

Another figure that repeatedly keeps surfacing in the D.C. Madam case is Vice President Dick Cheney, whose phone number while CEO of Halliburton appeared on numerous escort service lists. Friends close to Ms. Palfrey have told authorities that she was about to reveal more client names, and that this information was her ace-in-the-hole. In fact, Palfrey recently admitted, "Dick Cheney might be a client, but I can't tell you right now." There are few families powerful enough in our nation's capital to order a hit, but only days before her death, Palfrey complained to close associates that she was being followed, and that she feared a contract had been placed on her head. Such a notion is understandable, especially when Palfrey stated in August 1991—before being sentenced on similar charges—that she expected, "Rape, beating, maiming, disfigurement, and more than likely murder disguised in the form of just another jailhouse accident or suicide." Further, Palfrey assured numerous radio interviewers that she was not suicidal, and if she met a sudden demise, it would be murder.

A final twist to this story involves a former employee of Ms. Palfrey named Brandy Britton who, only three months earlier, also met an untimely death that was ruled a suicide—by hanging. With her trial set to start the following week, Britton threatened to blow the whistle and name names during her hearing. Palfrey had also warned that she planned on exposing the government and all those involved in her "erotic fantasy" call-girl ring.

If this data is correct and either Bill Clinton or Dick Cheney's names were contained in the D.C. Madam's little black book, the implications would be enormous. Hillary Clinton's presidential ambitions would be immediately sunk, while Cheney's inclusion on this list would be another black eye to an already disastrous, scandal-ridden Bush presidency. Unfortunately, more information will be difficult to obtain because the two main witnesses—Palfrey and Britton—are both dead. In addition, the DoJ has recently sealed the names of every client on this list, thereby protecting a multitude of skeletons that lurk in the closets of D.C.'s elite.

MAINSTREAM WON'T EXPOSE SORDID LIFESTYLES

After remaining in relative obscurity for over a decade, Monica Lewinsky's recent reemergence in *Vanity Fair* magazine and at a Philadelphia public speaking event has caused political pundits to speculate. As Bill Clinton's intern and adulterous lover inside the Oval Office, could this temptress who made blue dresses infamous actually benefit Hillary Clinton's 2016 bid for the White House?

Commentator Liz Cheney, daughter of former Vice President Cheney, thinks so. On May 8 she theorized, "I really wonder if [Lewinsky's *Vanity Fair* article] isn't an effort on the Clintons' part to get her story out of the way . . . so they can say its old news."

However, during an October 22, 2014 interview with this writer, historian Robert Morrow disagreed. "The more spotlights that are shined on Monica, the more it hurts the Clintons. They can't dismiss her story as irrelevant, especially when it leads to Bill and Hillary's rape and terror campaigns."

On this introductory note, Morrow turned his attention to the essential role that publications like AFP can play. "We know the national media will give Hillary a pass, so it's up to the alternative press to expose these two as the criminally minded codependent psychopaths that they are. Bill and Hillary have no shame or conscience and are willing to commit any type of crime and not care."

When asked how truth-seekers can spread this information, Morrow replied, "The Juanita Broaddrick interview on YouTube with NBC's Lisa Myers is hugely important. Viewers will understand how dangerous and toxic that interview is to the Clintons. NBC filmed it in 1999, but canned it for five weeks until Bill Clinton's Congressional impeachment trial was concluded. We need to spread this video around to millions of people."

For those unfamiliar with this sordid event, in 1978 Bill Clinton sexually attacked Ms. Broaddrick with such viciousness that he nearly bit off her lip. On January 20, 1999 NBC's Myers asked Broaddrick, "You're saying that Bill Clinton sexually assaulted you, that he raped you?"

Broaddrick's definitive, one word response was, "Yes."

In *Hillary (and Bill): The Sex Volume*, this writer chronicled how Myers told Broaddrick after the interview, "You're very, very credible."

Morrow commented, "The Clintons can't contain Lisa Myers' interview any longer. It's even worse for Hillary, a supposed feminist whose been covering up the actions of a sexual predator and rapist for 35 years."

Women should be particularly wary of Hillary, as Morrow outlined. "Because her husband's a lying sociopathic sex addict, Hillary continually referred to the women Bill attacked as prostitutes and sluts. In her eyes, his victims must be destroyed so that nobody believes them. She's some feminist, huh?"

Backing up his words, Morrow continued, "Bill Clinton sexually harassed Kathleen Willey in the White House. After Sally Perdue threatened to go public, Clinton thugs broke Perdue's Jeep window and placed a shotgun shell on her seat. Gennifer Flowers's house was broken into while Clinton cronies asked her neighbors, 'Is Gennifer the kind of person who'd commit suicide?'"

Even more troublesome for Hillary, Bill's philandering

isn't limited to the past. Morrow explained, "Bill's still cheating on Hillary, and has been for 40 years. In Ed Klein's latest book he detailed Bill's latest affair with a woman that Secret Service agents called the Energizer Bunny. Hillary knows her husband is a huge problem. Back in the '90s she threw a lamp at Bill's head. On another occasion in 1993, Hillary physically attacked him, leaving a huge gash on his face."

In conclusion, Morrow asked, "Is this what we want back in the White House, the Clintons with their phony, dysfunctional open-marriage?"

WILL HILLARY BE BILL'S FIXER AGAIN?

Although she's not directly implicated in the Jeffrey Epstein underage sex trafficking scandal, if her 2016 presidential aspirations stand any chance of getting off the ground, Hillary Clinton may be forced to once again fulfill her role as "fixer" to cover-up the criminal actions of husband Bill.

On January 15, 2015, this writer spoke with political historian Robert Morrow to get the inside scoop on this sordid story. "Jeffrey Epstein was, or still is, a billionaire," Morrow began, "who provided girls between the ages of 12 and 15 to VIP elites in politics, business, the media and Hollywood. Orgies were conducted at many of the houses Epstein owned all around the world, including Palm Beach, New Mexico, New York, and the Virgin Islands."

Offering details that other news outlets shy away from, Morrow continued, "We know who many of Epstein's pals were because his house manager in Palm Beach stole a contact book that was filled with names. This butler then circled the names of all those whom he considered to be pedophiles."

Here's where Bill Clinton enters the picture. According to Morrow, "Epstein's black book should be seen as a Holy Grail of sorts, and in it he listed 21 different ways of contacting Bill Clinton. These were personal phone numbers and email addresses that hardly anybody else in the world possessed. In addition, after Clinton left the White House, he made 17 trips with Epstein on his personal jet, 10 of those to what is known as Pedophile Island."

Certain that nobody misconstrues his words, Morrow clarified, "None of the girls who've gone public about Epstein being a pedophile-ringmaster have specifically named Bill Clinton, but one of their attorneys has implied that he pandered to underage girls. I see it as such: Bill Clinton was close friends with the biggest VIP pedophile peddler in the world. That's kind of like being friends with the biggest drug dealer in town."

That's why Hillary's talents become necessary. Morrow stressed, "Hillary Clinton is married to a rapist and serial sexual predator. Epstein contributed $25,000 to the Clinton Foundation after he'd been indicted in 2006. To me, that was Epstein's way of sending a message to Hillary saying, 'If you don't help me, I'll name all the women your husband had sex with.'"

Morrow further pursued this line of reasoning. "Hillary and Bill are part of a fake marriage. It's a political arrangement. She's been running off women for 40 years that could potentially get her husband in trouble. She even had her brothers doing it for her in Arkansas. Historically, Hillary has hired private investigators to initiate nasty terror campaigns against victims like Kathleen Willey and Sally Perdue. By portraying these women as 'nuts, sluts, and liars,' Hillary does anything she can to 'shut these bitches up.'"

Another element to this tale has surfaced, as Morrow related. "Epstein's number one recruiter of young women was a socialite named Ghislaine Maxwell, daughter of billionaire Robert Maxwell, whose corruption infuriated so many people that he was thrown overboard from his yacht and drowned in 1991. Ms. Maxwell considers herself close friends with Bill Clinton, even receiving an invitation to daughter Chelsea's wedding in 2010. Groomed as Epstein's pimp mama, Ghislaine opened doors for lots of VIPs, Prince Andrew being one of them. This scenario leads to a 17-year-old girl named Virginia Roberts, who asserts that she participated in an orgy with the prince and eight other women. By the way, Roberts also met on two separate occasions with Bill Clinton. Roberts made it perfectly clear what Epstein's associates were interested in: 'Fresh looking innocent girls not over 17 years old.'"

FEMINISTS IGNORE CLINTONS' WAR ON WOMEN

Would the American public allow Bill and Hillary Clinton back into the White House if they realized the full extent of their depravities? Roger Stone, coauthor of *The Clintons' War on Women* with Robert Morrow, seriously doubts it.

On October 22, 2015 during an interview with this writer, Stone described a sickening act. "When Bill Clinton raped Juanita Broaddrick, he used a signature disabling technique by biting his victim's upper lip. He's done the same thing to several other women in a bid to keep their mouths shut as he sexually assaulted them."

Stone filled in more details. "Women would be repulsed

if they knew what happened to Ms. Broaddrick when Bill Clinton almost bit through her lips. Afterward, her lips kept bleeding and turned black from his savagery."

In terms of Broaddrick's integrity, Stone offered this vote of confidence: "When NBC's Lisa Myers interviewed Broaddrick on January 20, 1999, she said, 'The good news is, you're credible.' Unfortunately, NBC execs kept this footage in the can for months until Clinton's impeachment hearing was concluded, despite Myers' arguments that it needed to be aired. Had they televised Broaddrick's claims before Congress voted, Clinton would have been impeached."

When this writer inquired as to why feminists and the National Organization of Women (NOW) persist in giving the Clintons a free pass, Stone replied, "In my experience, feminists to a person are liberals and Democrats first, and feminists second. They're very partisan-oriented. NOW refuses to respond to Bill's sexual crimes because they're dedicated to an agenda. Neither will you hear any news from the mainstream media about Bill's history as a sexual predator, or how Hillary has made a career of being his enabler."

Since it increasingly appears as if Hillary will win the Democratic Party nomination, Stone had some advice for GOP candidates: "Republicans need someone like Donald Trump who will stand on the debate stage beside Hillary and say: 'Your husband is a rapist, and you're his cover-up artist.' They have to quit being so polite. The key to beating Hillary comes by exposing Bill's behavior as a serial rapist and predator. He's someone that's as bad as Bill Cosby."

Stone offered additional ideas. "Another woman that Bill targeted was Kathleen Willey. In a profound way, she's gone on the record stating that Hillary's the one engaging in a war on women. After going public about how Bill sexually molested her in the White House, Willey's house was broken into and ransacked, her windshield smashed, and she was assaulted on a jogging path. One of Willey's pets was also killed, plus she received late night phone calls threatening her children. All of these dirty tricks were verifiably linked to a Hillary associate named Jack Palladino."

There exist further hypocrisies that Stone pointed out: "No place where Hillary was ever the boss did women receive the same pay as men. Plus, it's incredible how much money flows into the Clinton Foundation from places that horribly oppress women. In these countries, women can't vote, they're not allowed to drive cars, and in Muslim countries under Sharia law, if a woman claims that she was raped, oftentimes she's stoned to death. Yet, the Clintons still gladly receive dirty money from these places."

Not surprisingly, the Clintons fear these revelations, as Stone described: "Hillary is very afraid of this book. Her press secretary, Brian Fallon, has created a war room to specifically discredit this book and any other which exposes their crimes."

FEMINISTS, HILLARY WAGE REAL WAR ON WOMEN

Hillary Clinton portrays herself as a guiding light of women's rights, a cause she'll undoubtedly exploit as a candidate for president in the 2016 election.

However, considering her role as an enabler and cover-up artist for her sexual predator husband, many critics are beginning to question whether Mrs. Clinton and her legion of feminist supporters are the true source of what Democrats called a

"war on women" during the 2012 campaign season. To bolster
their point, strategists trotted out a graduate student named Sandra Fluke who complained that Republicans hated women because they didn't want to pay for their birth control pills.

This controversial issue gained momentum on February
16, 2014 when Kathleen Willey, a former volunteer aide that
Bill Clinton sexually harassed in the Oval Office, stated during
a radio interview, "Hillary Clinton is the war on women."

Two days later, during a televised interview, Willey became more adamant, telling Megyn Kelly of Fox News,
"Hillary Clinton ruins women before they can ruin Bill . . .
I found out firsthand how she operates . . . Hillary choreo-
graphed every terror campaign that has been waged against
women. Bill Clinton groped me in the Oval Office against
my will, and I've been harassed and intimidated for years . .
. How could she be a champion of women's rights and do
what she does to women? Hillary needs to be exposed." Willey went on to describe how her car had been vandalized
and beloved pets mysteriously went missing in an attempt
to bully her.

According to victim Juanita Broaddrick, Clinton "forcibly,
painfully raped her" while nearly biting her lip off to prevent
her from screaming. Also, Governor Clinton dispatched state
troopers to procure Arkansas state employee Paula Jones,
who they escorted to a hotel room. Moments later, Clinton
exposed himself while trying to strong-arm Jones into committing an unmentionable act.

This theme of predatory behavior can likewise be found in
Willey's description of Clinton's assault on her in the White
House. "[His] sexual approach came out of nowhere and was
forceful, almost to the point of an attack." Saddest of all, Willey

reached out to President Clinton on the day her husband committed suicide. This was the treatment she received in return.

It goes without saying that an authentic advocate of women's rights would try to have serial rapists arrested and imprisoned. Yet Hillary, concerned only with power and political expediency, established secret police smear campaigns against her husband's victims. Moreover, she formed covert spy networks, hired private detectives to intimidate women that threatened to go public, and even urged her thuggish brother to "take out" one of Bill's bludgeoned casualties.

Hillary's tactics also extended to verbal abuse. She referred to women who were sexually assaulted as "bimbo eruptions," "white trash" and "cheap sluts." Plus, who could forget Hillary's hit man James Carville's comment about Paula Jones? "Drag a $100 bill through a trailer park and you'll never know what you'll find," Carville snidely remarked. Quite a compassionate stance from those who proclaim to be defenders of abused women.

On February 17-18, 2014, this writer contacted eight different feminist and/or women's anti-sexual violence organizations to elicit a response to this situation. Amazingly, not a single one of these groups agreed to speak about Hillary and Bill's war on women. One of the only comments came from Marsha Roberson, director of communications for Futures without Violence, which attempts to educate women on all forms of violence. Robertson stated, "We don't tend to get involved with candidates or day-to-day politics. It's not like there's a cover-up. This issue simply hasn't risen to the level of priority yet."

That's like saying an organization devoted to preventing arson doesn't think it's a priority when two dozen homes had been deliberately burned to the ground.

This same blasé attitude arose from a staff member at Advocates for Human Rights, an organization that ironically tries to strengthen accountability mechanisms against those who prey on females. This woman told this writer, "We don't comment on specific politicians or candidates." If her rationale applies across the board, anybody elected to public office could go on a rampage like Ted Bundy and they'd remain silent. In all honesty, why are these groups even in existence if they refuse to address the most prolific serial rapist in American political history, along with his handler wife who actively engages in vendettas against those who've suffered from his abuses?

On the other hand, Laura Wood, a blogger known as "The Thinking Housewife," issued this statement to this writer on February 19, 2014. "Hillary Clinton's the Chairman Mao of feminism. If Bill had been a Republican senator, he would have lost his career a long time ago. Instead, his bad behavior is viewed as a personal failing that has nothing to do with politics. The ends justify the means."

In this writer's book *Hillary (and Bill): The Sex Volume*, Hillary's antics are exposed in graphic detail.

SCANDALS CREATE CHAOS FOR DEMOCRATIC PARTY

If FBI investigators uncover evidence of criminal wrongdoing in Hillary Clinton's use of a private email server to send classified government material (assuming, of course, that it hasn't already been scrubbed), could the charges force her out of the 2016 presidential race? If so, what type of turmoil would this move create within the Democratic Party, especially in terms of finding a new candidate to replace her?

Plus, will a host of other scandals surrounding the Clintons be exposed, adding even more pandemonium to this precarious situation?

Jamison Faught of the Muskogee, Oklahoma Tea Party thinks so. During an August 13, 2015 interview, Faught told this writer, "If Hillary is forced out it'll be chaos beyond anything the Democrats have ever seen, possibly even leading to a brokered convention next summer. Honestly, though, I don't think Clinton will drop out unless she's carried away in handcuffs."

Faught continued, "The Democrats are definitely scared. In 2008, Hillary was their anointed candidate, the one expected to be their nominee. But she's more vulnerable now than seven years ago, none the least because of all the unanswered questions surrounding Benghazi. People simply don't trust her, and the Democrats know it. That's why they're searching for someone without all the baggage."

Amid a plethora of rumors as to who might jump into the race, Faught ascertained, "If you look at all the names being mentioned to potentially replace Hillary, you have Joe Biden, Al Gore, John Kerry, and even Governor Jerry Brown. Democrats keep looking back into the past. They don't have any fresh faces or new ideas."

As to the diminishing number of liberals that support Hillary, Faught observed, "The only ones still onboard are those with a blind loyalty to the Clintons or the Democratic machine. They favor her over the safety of our country. If anyone else would have put that much sensitive information out there, they'd be sitting in jail right now. The FBI would have showed up at their doorstep and arrested them. How could anyone look at Hillary and think she'd make our country better?"

Other crushing scandals could also undermine the Clintons. Well-known author and feminist cultural critic Camille Paglia has compared Bill Clinton to comedian Bill Cosby. To date, 57 women have accused Cosby of drugging and raping them. In this same vein, Kathleen Willey, who Clinton sexually molested in the Oval Office on November 29, 1993 following her husband's suicide, has launched a website that encourages women who've been victimized by Clinton's predatory behavior to step forward. If dozens of women band together as they have against Cosby, the Clintons would face a rash of extremely negative publicity, particularly among their feminist base.

Similarly, former *Washington Post* investigative journalist Ronald Kessler claimed on July 29 that not only is Bill still philandering like in the olden days, but "[Their marriage] is a business relationship. It's a total fake, like everything else about Hillary. It's a big show and a scam."

Also on July 29, 2015 in a public statement made at a Washington, D.C. federal courthouse, Linda Tripp, the woman who exposed Bill's affair with Monica Lewinsky, stated, "His political success was largely dependent on Hillary. He owed her a great deal. As is widely acknowledged, Hillary took care of all the 'bimbo eruptions,' of which there were thousands, in order to present to the world an electable candidate. In this endeavor she was ruthless. She destroyed women so that their stories never saw the light of day."

In regard to Hillary's honesty, or lack thereof, Tripp announced, "I watched her on countless occasions blatantly lie to the American people, [and] this was not a mistake or error or even spin. This was pure manipulation of the truth."

Money

CLINTON CRONIES SCHOOL OBAMA

The Wall Street elite have found a friend in Barack Obama. On multiple occasions, Barack Obama promised the American public that his administration would not only investigate and track down those responsible for systematic fraud that led to America's 2008 financial collapse, but also prosecute and imprison them. To date, in the eighth year of his presidency, not a single Wall Street banker has been arrested, let alone jailed.

Obama and former Attorney General Eric Holder's refusal to act against those involved in serious financial crimes was twofold: First, three of Obama's top seven contributors in 2008 were Goldman Sachs, Citigroup, and JPMorgan Chase & Co. Secondly, many in Obama's cabinet are precisely the same individuals that coerced President Bill Clinton into deregulating Wall Street by repealing the Depression-era Glass-Steagall Act while also permitting an array of financial institutions to merge into mega-entities that became "too big to fail."

The four primary individuals moving from the Clinton

to Obama administrations were (a) John Podesta, Obama's special advisor, (b) Gene Sperling, director of Obama's National Economic Council, and (c) Bo Cutter, an integral member of Obama's transition committee. It must also be remembered that Eric Holder served under Clinton's Attorney General Janet Reno.

A final, even more influential man, Robert Rubin, engineered Wall Street deregulation under Bill Clinton. Before acting as Clinton's first Treasury Secretary, Rubin spent 26 years at Goldman Sachs. Later, he became Citigroup's chairman. Both of these financial titans were top dollar donors to Obama.

The importance of this revolving door between Clinton and Obama can be found in an April 1, 2014 quote by liberal journalist Eric Zeusse. "Bill Clinton deregulated Wall Street so that unregulated derivatives-trading and megabanks could defraud outside investors and deceive homebuyers, [thus] bringing the economy to collapse under George W. Bush. Barack Obama has the record of zero prosecutions of these banksters."

To obtain further insights, on April 24, 2014 this writer contacted Darrell Castle, a 2008 vice presidential candidate for the Constitution Party. When posed with the incestuous ties that extended from Clinton to Obama, Castle explained, "Obama had only been a senator for one-and-a-half years before running for president. Somebody had to point him in the right direction to find the bankers, and these people were the Clintons."

In terms of the disappointment felt by those who believed in his mantra of hope and change, Castle provided this stark analysis. "A lot of Obama's supporters on the left realize he's a pawn of Wall Street. Liberals no longer expect anything from Obama because he's never delivered on his promises."

Along this same line of thought, Castle added, "Obama's ties to the Clintons confirm something that I've suspected for a long time. They're all in it together. There's a long grey line which passes from one administration to another. After all, the Federal Reserve printing trillions of dollars under Obama is meant to do only one thing: pump up Wall Street. Obviously, Obama and Wall Street are closely related."

Castle found another aspect of this president quite disturbing. "Obama constantly rails against the 1%, yet he's the worst offender. His hypocrisy bothers me. Middle class income is shrinking or in full retreat. Regardless, there's something disgusting about he and his wife's ostentatious displays of wealth. For them to flaunt the high-life means they have no understanding of everyday Americans who work for a living."

To close, Castle said, "Obama has no intention of reinstating Glass-Steagall, and it's traceable back to the Clintons."

FINANCIAL JUGGERNAUT MUST BE STOPPED

Hillary (and Bill): The *Sex, Drugs* and *Murder* volumes by this writer illustrate in graphic detail why neither of the Clintons should ever again be allowed into the White House. Still, with millions in her political war chest and liberal media advocates pushing the intrigue of our nation's first female president, many pundits predict that Hillary could return to 1600 Pennsylvania Avenue in 2016.

"Bill and Hillary are consummate fundraisers. People open their wallets whenever they show up. Not only in politics, but also with the Clinton Global Initiative (CGI) and the fees obtained for their speeches. Money trails them wherever they go."

Dean Levinthal, manager of the Center for Public Integrity's federal political team, spoke these words to this writer during a July 8, 2014 interview. He continued, "With Bill and Hillary, you have a former president, governor, senator, secretary of state and first lady. They're the most powerful political couple in U.S. history. Their arsenal of financial resources and army of supporters extends back to the 1970s."

As for the 2016 election, Levinthal noted, "Hillary's Super Political Action Committees have already raised millions, and her donor lists are almost endless. Add to that various non-profit organizations, unions, corporations, special interest groups and billionaires pouring untold amounts of money into her coffers. The sky's the limit for her political fundraising."

Levinthal further explained, "The Supreme Court's 2010 *Citizens United* decision [i.e., the government cannot restrict contributions made by independent entities] was a game-changer. It's absolutely frightening that a candidate can raise and spend as much money as they want. Some call it legalized political corruption. For 2016, Hillary can call in all her political chits and bring to bear an overwhelming amount of campaign firepower. It's the way of politics today, making it that much more difficult for any other Democratic candidate to oppose her."

Other matters concerning dollars and cents have raised eyebrows. Namely, CGI, started in 1997, raised $492 million by 2013. Yet, from 2007-2008 this so-called non-profit organization racked up a $40 million deficit. In 2012 the Clinton's cash cow tallied another $8 million deficit despite totaling $214 million in revenues. With a $17 trillion national debt looming over this nation, Hillary's inability to balance the books should concern every taxpayer.

Moreover, charges of crony capitalism and influence peddling with shady corporations, government officials and unscrupulous donors plague the Clintons. *The New York Time's* Wynton Hall wrote on August 14, 2013, "As of 2008, the Clinton Foundation raised at least $46 million from Saudi Arabia, Kuwait, Qatar, Brunei, Oman and other foreign governments."

Obviously, these numbers transpired before Hillary became secretary of state. So, who's to say that when Hillary cut deals for foreign aid with narco-states like Afghanistan, millions weren't clandestinely funneled into her own bank account at CGI?

Interestingly, during her tenure as secretary of state from 2009-2010, funds from the U.S. Agency for International Development (USAID) to Afghanistan skyrocketed from $470 million to $1.4 billion. Considering the unprecedented levels of fraud under President Hamid Karzai, nobody can be assured that these allotments were properly used. On April 21, 2014, political news reporter Richard Berkow confirmed these suspicions. "Confidential 2012 and 2013 USAID memos show that none of the seven Afghan ministries receiving money could be trusted to spend it effectively." The person responsible for securing these transactions to Afghanistan was Hillary Clinton.

Kickbacks from official sources aren't the only resources potentially being deposited into CGI's money pit. When controversies ensued about Hillary receiving $200,000 per speaking engagement, she rebutted these criticisms by claiming that many of the fees were donated to a worthwhile cause—CGI.

Also, what prevents the Clintons from conveniently pledging substantial amounts of resources to areas where they need votes in 2016? CGI has already been accused of Chicago-style pay-to-play tactics with certain developers and philanthropists in order to redirect payments that could be used to build new malls, hospitals, or green energy initiatives. Hillary could then tout these projects as a way of garnering more votes in economically depressed areas.

This one-hand-washing-the-other ploy even extends to Hillary's recent $14 million advance from publisher Simon & Schuster, Inc. for her biography *Hard Choices*. Selling 160,000 copies to date at a cover price of $35, total sales only reached $2.4 million. Compared to the $14 million she's already pocketed, was this arrangement nothing more than an illegal campaign contribution disguised as an author's advance?

In light of Hillary's past windfall from cattle futures where she turned a $1,000 investment into $100,000, the *Journal of Economics and Finance* concluded the odds of such an occurrence were 1 in 31 trillion. Amid cries of bribery and conflict of interest, nothing with this woman is beyond the realm of dirty tricks and underhanded schemes.

HILLARY'S WALL STREET LOVEFEST

Hillary Clinton switches her political hyperbole more often than she changes hairstyles. In the past, she's complained about a vast right-wing conspiracy, bimbo eruptions, and how the Benghazi massacre "doesn't really matter at this point."

Today, all of a sudden, Hillary has transformed into a populist. During a May 16 speech at the New America Foundation, Clinton derided robber barons and the shadow banking system. On the surface, her words may placate those who put stock in empty rhetoric.

In actuality, though, Hillary has never opposed the money cabal. To the contrary, she and Bill collaborated with them every step of the way during their 40-year political careers. Since Hillary left her post as Secretary of State in 2013, she's raked in over $5 million giving speeches to the likes of Goldman Sachs, neocon warmongers at the Carlyle Group, and private equity fat cats from Kohlberg Kravis Roberts. As this writer previously noted, Hillary pocketed $400,000 alone from two speeches at Goldman Sachs.

On June 4, 2014 this writer contacted historian Robert Morrow. When asked about the significance of Hillary's hobnobbing with the Wall Street banking elite, Morrow began, "Goldman Sachs has always been a key player at Bilderberg. In 1991 Bill Clinton attended a Bilderberg meeting in Baden-Baden, Germany. After receiving their approval, the following year he became President of the United States."

Morrow added, "The Clintons turned their administration over to Wall Street cronies like Robert Rubin, Lawrence Summers, and Roger Altman. Democrats have always enjoyed strong ties with investment bankers, and the Clintons are the biggest culprits of all."

As our conversation turned specifically to Mrs. Clinton, Morrow proffered, "Hillary is a phony populist. The reason Wall Street invests in her boils down to influence peddling. They see the Clintons as Democratic royalty who've always surrounded themselves with wealthy investment banker friends. Hillary has never deviated away from being pro-Federal Reserve, pro-endless war, and pro-big government."

Proving this point, on June 6, 2014 Hillary attended another Goldman Sachs function in Manhattan under the guise of her CGI. It goes without saying that in 2008, Citigroup and Goldman Sachs were Clinton's two largest campaign donors during her failed presidential bid.

On May 21, 2014 Rutgers University political scientist Russ Baker made a startling admission. "[Hillary] is basically part of the Wall Street wing of the Democratic Party." Those who doubt this assessment should realize that in the seven years after Bill and Hillary left the White House they epitomized 1% excess by amassing $109 million. Quite simply, these limousine liberals are more accustomed to backroom deals, insider trading, political patronage, and dirty money than they are to the hardships of extended unemployment and feeding one's children in a stagnant economy.

Considering that Wall Street has historically championed the war machine, investigative reporter Glenn Greenwald, who broke the Edward Snowden-National Security Agency spy scandal, seethed with disdain at the thought of another Clinton presidency. On May 12, 2014 he remarked, "She's a [expletive deleted] hawk, like a neocon practically. She's surrounded by all these sleazy money types who are corrupting everything everywhere."

POOR-MOUTH ROUTINE FALLS FLAT

Like a modern-day Marie Antoinette sarcastically urging her peasants to eat cake, Hillary Clinton feigns poverty, all the while amassing—along with her husband Bill—$109 million over the past 14 years.

During a June 25, 2015 interview, Tim Graham, director of media analysis at the Media Research Center, told this writer, "Hillary Clinton telling ABC's Diane Sawyer that they were "dead broke" when leaving the White House is beyond ludicrous. These are people that are millionaires a hundred times over."

Graham added, "Hillary should meet with assembly line workers and explain how she makes $200,000 per speech. You can't convince average Americans that you're poor after pulling down these kinds of six-figure sums."

Providing one other essential point, Graham stated to this writer, "Hillary accepted an $8 million book bonus before she ever joined the U.S. Senate in 2001. To say she was dead-broke is simply not true. The reason they were in debt was because of legal defense bills."

On June 25, 2015 during an interview, Bob Porto of the Arkansas Pulaski County Tea Party carried this assertion a step further. "People don't buy this woe-is-me approach. Bill and Hillary Clinton were in debt because they had to pay off the legal costs incurred from lawsuits associated with Bill's philandering."

Being an Arkansas resident, Porto remembers well the shenanigans that transpired three decades ago. "When Bill was governor, the Clintons never owned any property in Arkansas. They always fed off the state's breast milk. They lived off political welfare. Now Hillary has decided to cash in. I think in her mind Hillary looks at all the time she supposedly sacrificed for our country. Now she has to make up for it financially. The big question is: considering all of Hillary and Bill's political connections, what did they have to offer to get $109 million in return?"

Sylvia Curry of the Arkansas White Hall Tea Party Patriots also spoke with this writer on June 25, 2015. She began, "I could tell you some stories about those two when they lived in Arkansas. Imagine the snobbishness to infer that they're poor when Hillary owns two mansions and wants $225,000 for speaking at universities. Yesterday, Bill Clinton said that he and Hillary make it a point at least once a month to visit the grocery store on weekends and speak with regular people."

After laughing at the absurdity of this proposition, Curry continued, "Do you remember when Hillary stole publicly owned furniture from the White House and had to be forced into returning it? Then, a few days ago their daughter Chelsea suggested that she doesn't care about money. If I lived in a $6 million apartment and made $600,000 a year from NBC News, I wouldn't care about money either. What do these statements say about the Clinton's perspective on the real America? I think Hillary's arrogance has turned plenty of people against her."

Even Hillary's most ardent supporters are vexed by her gaffes. On June 23, 2015 former South Carolina Democratic Party chairman Dick Harpootlian lamented, "I don't know whether it's that she's been 'Madame Secretary' for so long, but [Hillary's] generating an imperial image. She's been living 30, going on 40 years, with somebody bringing her coffee every morning. It's more 'Downtown Abbey' [a television show about England's Royal Family] than it is America."

HILLARY BREAKS FUNDRAISING RECORD

It's a fact: Mega-bankers, huge corporations and Big Media padded Mrs. Clinton's pockets in 2015. Hillary Clinton, who falsely attempts to portray herself as a woman whose interests lie with everyday workers and the common man, raised over $45 million during the first quarter of her 2015 presidential campaign. It should be noted that the largest single donors were comprised of banks, corporate law firms, media conglomerates, and a leading abortion rights organization. Although specific totals won't be released until mid-July, Clinton's top 10 donors from 1999-2015 included Citigroup, Goldman Sachs, JPMorgan Chase & Co., Time Warner, Lehman Brothers, and Morgan Stanley. Financial experts doubt that this trend will be broken with Clinton's current campaign.

Publically available records also reveal that during her tenure as a New York Senator and while Secretary of State under Barack Obama, influence peddlers such as foreign governments, the lending titan Freddie Mac, and major construction firms that needed favors all contributed large sums of money to the Clinton coffers. In addition, millions more were funneled into Hillary and Bill's so-called "non-profit charity." Bill Allison, a senior fellow at a government watchdog group called the Sunlight Foundation, stated on June 10, 2015, "It seems like the Clinton Foundation operates as a slush fund for the Clintons."

Indeed, Hillary's fundraising efforts even surpassed the record set by Barack Obama in the first quarter of 2011 when he raised $41.9 million. During the opening three months of 2015, Mrs. Clinton also staged a whopping 58 high profile fundraisers across the country that generated at least $23 million.

On July 8, 2015 this writer contacted Pam Stout of the Sandpoint Idaho Tea Party Patriots. Stout was not only featured as the subject of a February 15, 2010 *New York Times* front page article, she also made an appearance on the David

Letterman Show a month later.

In terms of Clinton's status as a stellar money-making machine, especially in regard to funds received from leading financial houses and Wall Street corporations, Stout said, "The donations speak for themselves. If Clinton really planned on reigning in these entities, they wouldn't be giving her all this money. There's so much cronyism involved in her campaign that it borders on fascism."

When asked about the Clinton Foundation, Stout replied, "I don't believe this is truly a non-profit foundation because I haven't seen them doing a lot of great work. All they do is raise money, with only a small percentage of the funds going to specific causes. The foundation doesn't do what they say they do. How much money goes to their executives? It's obvious that you can pull a lot of money out of a foundation. This lady has no morals. All she wants is power."

Then there's the issue of quid pro quo favors being traded within the foundation, a technique that both Hillary and Obama learned in their corrupt hometown of Chicago. Stout ascertained. "There's a total conflict of interest for Hillary at the foundation. It's easy to understand why certain corporations would want her in the White House. She'll make life a lot easier for them, and the more promises she makes, the more money she'll raise."

Anyone that doubts this assessment should examine the Clinton's boondoggle in Haiti. Critics claim that over $10 billion was stolen via kickbacks between the foundation and a pseudo-non-governmental organization named the Haiti Reconstruction Commission.

Foreign Policy

HILLARY THE REAL FOREIGN POLICY PRESIDENT?

Hs Secretary of State and one-time Bilderberg attendee Hillary Clinton actually the Obama administration's hands-on president, just as she was the de facto governor and president during her husband's tenure in Arkansas and Washington, D.C.?

Doubters should be reminded of a February 24, 2008 quote delivered by Barack Obama during a campaign stop in Lorain, Ohio. "She [Hillary] has essentially presented herself as co-president during the Clinton years."

Obama knew full well of what he spoke. Journalist Scott Creighton's March 19, 2011 article, "President Hillary Clinton's Shock and Awe," began with this stark contrast. "While Hillary Clinton met with 22 world leaders to decide the fate of Libya, they kept Barack Obama in the back of the bus and let the real president take the lead." Creighton also pointed out that while Obama golfed and vacationed, Hillary conferred with practically every world leader and dignitary imaginable.

A quick glance at the State Department's travel itinerary reveals nearly 75 trips to foreign countries by Clinton where the real groundwork for a New World Order super-structure was being laid.

While some commentators call Hillary a "Globalist Grand Wizard," her influence also spread to the formation of Obama's cabinet after his 2008 election. In a March 18, 2012 article, Edward Ulrich wrote, "31 of the 47 people Barack Obama has named for appointments have ties to the Clinton administration, including Eric Holder, Larry Summers, Rahm Emanuel and Timothy Geithner."

To get a better idea of Hillary's modus operandi, in a 2006 film entitled *Inside Man*, Hollywood actress Jodie Foster analyzed her character's role in remedying delicate situations. "She's a fixer, a rich Madison Avenue lawyer who fixes things when they go wrong. Say you were a mayor and you got caught in bed with three dead hookers, I would be brought in to fix the situation." When asked how her character did it, Foster replied, "Call in lots of favors. You use people and kind of puppet behind the scenes, manipulate them. She's a dubious bad guy."

The above words perfectly describe Hillary Clinton's entire political career. In fact, *Hillary (and Bill): The Murder Volume* contains the following passage. "Hillary acted as an enabler and fixer to cover-up for her husband's serial philandering and sexual reign of terror."

But being a handler for Bill's raging libido was minor compared to Hillary's role in trafficking drugs through Mena Airport, the cover-up of Vince Foster and Ron Brown's murders, "ChinaGate," and laundering money through the Arkansas Development Finance Authority (ADFA) to finance their campaigns.

Learning the ropes from Washington, D.C.'s former fixer

extraordinaire—longtime Bilderberg luminary Vernon Jordan—Hillary has always nurtured a comfortable relationship with Wall Street bankers and the Council on Foreign Relations (CFR). Indeed, during a July 17, 2009 CFR address, Hillary revealed, "We get a lot of advice from the Council, so this will mean I won't have as far to go to be told what we should be doing and how we should think about the future."

With the Obama administration pursuing a number of globalist treaties that undermine American sovereignty, it's clear that Hillary Clinton is the driving force behind these moves as she travels from country to country. According to the elitists' worldview, individuals should be subordinate and powerless to collectivists, while nationalists are viewed as a distraction to be folded into the globalist whole.

GUN-RUNNING:
FROM 'FAST AND FURIOUS' TO LIBYA & SYRIA

Continuing the tradition of U.S. arms trafficking to Afghani *mujahideen*, Contras in Central America, and agitators who overthrew Muammar Qadaffi, it appears as if U.S. Ambassador to Libya Chris Stevens' primary role in Benghazi was as a liaison to dispatch weapons from Libya through Turkey into Syria. There, rebels used this firepower in a continuing campaign to topple Syrian President Bashar al-Assad.

During an October 24, 2012 interview, Scott Creighton, a blogger touting himself as an "American Everyman," told this writer, "Stevens was a gunrunner and paymaster whose job was to destabilize Libya so that the U.S. could control the aftermath." In a September 24, 2012 article, Creighton wrote, "It was the CIA and Stevens working together in Libya since early

2011 who created and ran the fake revolution in the first place."

Former CIA asset Claire Lopez expanded on this operation in an October 18, 2012 commentary. "Earlier in 2012 President Obama signed an intelligence finding to permit the CIA and other U.S. government agencies to provide support to Syrian rebels." She continued, "Reports that those rebels now have surface-to-air missiles call to mind the thousands of such weapons looted from Qadaffi's stockpiles during and after the revolt that ousted him in October 2011."

Not only did Stevens use Benghazi as a stronghold for his gun-walking mission and to recruit mercenaries who fought against Assad, on September 6, 2012 a Libyan ship hauling 400 tons of cargo docked in Iskenderun, Turkey. Among the freight later smuggled across the border were rocket-propelled grenades and heat-seeking missiles that were subsequently used to down Syrian jetfighters.

On October 24, 2012 Russian General Nikolai Makarov weighed in on this tense situation. "We have reliable information that Syrian militants have foreign portable anti-aircraft missile systems, including those made in the USA."

FAST AND FURIOUS: THE REAL STORY

One evening before the midterm elections, when every mainstream media outlet was focusing on candidates and ballot counts, Eric Holder's Department of Justice surreptitiously dumped 64,280 previously unreleased Fast and Furious documents in the dead of night. The operation known as Fast and Furious involved Bureau of Alcohol, Tobacco, Firearms and Explosives (ATF or BATFE) agents coercing gun dealers from southwestern states into selling thousands of semi-automatic weapons to known Mexican drug cartels. Coincidentally, those weapons allowed to walk across the border were the exact same ones that Obama, Holder, and Secretary of State Hillary Clinton sought to make illegal under an assault weapons ban.

These Fast and Furious files, many of them still heavily redacted, are considered so explosive that Obama defaulted to a rarely used legal move known as 'executive privilege' in hopes of protecting Holder, the nation's first Attorney General held in criminal contempt by Congress.

Further proof that smoking guns exist within these reports arose when Darrell Issa (R-Ca.) acknowledged that, due to highly sensitive information, these documents wouldn't be publicly released. Moreover, despite several federal lawsuits, thousands of Fast and Furious pages are still being concealed by the Obama White House. Many of them allegedly relate to Holder's direct complicity in overseeing this operation, his crafting of deceptive talking points, and how he knowingly perjured himself when testifying before Congress. Ironically, on October 21, 2014 Holder confessed to reporters that his biggest regret as Attorney General stemmed from an inability to pass gun control legislation.

Seeking some straight answers, on November 5, 2014 this writer interviewed Robert Farago, founder of an organization known as "The Truth about Guns." When asked about the real story behind Fast and Furious, Farago began, "The government wants us to believe Fast and Furious was a sting operation gone wrong, but that explanation makes no sense at all because law enforcement didn't keep track of the guns going into Mexico. In fact, ATF agents were specifically told to let these weapons go without any supervision."

After debunking that angle, Farago continued, "Another theory involves a conspiracy to enact gun control laws. In other words, these guns went south and would then be found at crime scenes. Thus, Holder's people would say America needs an assault weapons ban. ATF agents actually high-fived one another after learning Fast and Furious guns were located in Mexico."

Still, this line of reasoning doesn't reach the crux of the issue. According to Farago, "Most Fast and Furious guns went to the Sinaloa drug cartel. They're at war with another cartel, the Zetas. What Obama and Holder desperately don't want the American public to learn is that they were favoring the Sinaloa cartel and allowing them to smuggle guns and drugs into our country. Furthermore, there was also a Sinaloan money-walking scandal where millions of dollars were being smuggled into America and laundered between the various parties involved."

Without hedging his bets, Farago insisted, "Under Fast and Furious, the Obama administration allowed guns and drugs to go south into Mexico in exchange for the Sinaloa cartel's shipment of drugs north. They were in bed with this cartel, and all kinds of agencies assisted in the operation, including Hillary Clinton's State Department, the Drug Enforcement Administration, CIA, and Border Control. We're talking about highly illegal arms trafficking, an international crime. For Obama, Fast and Furious is an impeachable offense."

Farago backed-up his claims. "Here's what we know. First, the head of ATF, Ken Melson, watched guns 'walk' via CCTV cameras. Second, ATF special agent John Dodson told his men to stand-down and let the guns go. Third, ATF never monitored these weapons or tried to recover them. There were also no arrests or any investigations. Holder and the ATF knew their guns went into the hands of cartel members. They were actively helping the Sinaloa cartel by aiding the flow of guns, money and drugs back and forth across our southern border. The Obama administration helped the bad guys who were supplying drugs to America."

Strangely, in the beginning Holder and company deemed their Fast and Furious operation a success. That was until a pivotal event changed everything. Farago filled in the details. "We know for a fact that Holder was involved in Fast and Furious, but once Border Agent Brian Terry was murdered, the whole thing blew wide open. At that moment Holder went into cover-up mode. Since he knew what was happening, it's certain that Obama did too."

Fitting a final piece to the puzzle, Farago told this writer, "Brian Terry was shot with a gun provided to the bad guys by his own government, and our president has sold him out. Terry was a man who genuinely believed in his mission to protect our border against illegal aliens. But did you know that Obama's Department of Homeland Security head Janet Napolitano only allowed her border patrol agents to carry bean bag ammo? So, when a team of U.S. border agents, including Terry, confronted a gang of criminals, they shot bean bag ammunition at them. Their adversaries returned fire with AK-47s and killed Terry. That's how he got murdered."

HILLARY'S LIBYAN DECEPTIONS HAUNT HER

Hillary Clinton is in a conundrum. She wants to be president, yet while serving as secretary of state from 2009-2013, those in the highest seats of government so distrusted her that they established their own back-channel intelligence networks to sidestep blatantly false disinformation emanating from the State Department. Specifically, Pentagon officials, as well as Representative Dennis Kucinich (D-Ohio), the Joint Chiefs of Staff (JCS), and DIA realized that Mrs. Clinton's lies leading up to the U.S.-NATO invasion of Libya in 2011 were so egregious that they needed to counter them with legitimate input.

Regrettably, a passive, insulated, absentee President Obama listened to only the women surrounding him, namely Hillary Clinton, UN Ambassador Susan Rice, National Security Council member Samantha Power, and chief advisor Valerie Jarrett. Obama's dismissal of all other contrary data reached such pathetic levels that he privately whispered to Democratic loyalists that Libya was entirely in Secretary Clinton's hands.

While Hillary, along with Senator John McCain (R-Ariz.), Senator Lindsey Graham (R-S.C.), Senator John Kerry (D-Mass.) and French President Nicolas Sarkozy rabidly pushed for an invasion against Muammar Qadaffi, Obama sat listlessly, letting the neocons and militaristic women in his cabinet push America into another unnecessary war.

Those opposing this senseless attack on Libya—Kucinich, Defense Secretary Robert Gates, and JCS Chairman Admiral Mike Mullen—were denied access to the Oval Office, had their phone calls ignored, or faced a wall of denial in terms of trying to negotiate a settlement with Libya. Meanwhile, Clinton, akin to Bush-Cheney warmongers that fabricated a weapons of mass destruction fable in Iraq, funneled falsified reports to the White House claiming that Qadaffi intended to commit mass genocidal crimes against his citizens.

Desperate to halt Clinton's quest for Libyan regime change, Kucinich, along with the Pentagon, privately contacted a number of insiders in Tripoli. They soon learned through their liaisons that not only had Clinton been falsifying reports, she spewed outright lies about impending Rwanda-style mass exterminations.

Of course, as AFP readers know, Clinton's grand designs involved more than Qadaffi's removal. She and her covert arms dealers were also trafficking weapons to al-Qaeda-linked rebels. Worse, they used the U.S. consulate in Benghazi to transport surface-to-air missiles, tanks, rifles and ammunition through Turkey to forces fighting against Syrian President Bashar al-Assad. As a result of this penchant for war in Libya that was engineered by Clinton and the Obama administration, the Middle East is now further enflamed by Islamic jihadists that go by names like ISIS.

Seeking other perspectives on this matter, on February 5 this writer contacted Matt Mattingly of Maine's 6th District Tea Party. When asked about the skepticism associated with Clinton's dishonesty, Mattingly replied, "When we look at all she's done as secretary of state, all I can think of is the Peter Principle which states that people rise to their level of incompetence. I view Clinton in the same vein as Obama. They both have a huge disconnect from situations that are developing on the ground. Benghazi is a perfect example. It can't give people much confidence that she'd do any better as commander-in-chief than she did as secretary of state."

Likewise, on that same day, this writer spoke with Robert Shannon, who was one of the original founders of two Virginia tea party groups. In terms of the Libyan invasion, Shannon surmised, "I think the defense industry and Wall Street have sunk their tentacles so deeply into the body politic that, if you connect the dots, you'll find a straight line from K Street lobbyists going to top-tier elected officials like Clinton. If it serves their political aspirations, the Clintons will open the spigots and take money from anyone."

THE OBAMA-CLINTON SHADOW GOVERNMENTS

Ever since the JFK assassination, whenever "conspiracy theorists" mentioned shadow governments or hidden hands that controlled political affairs, their counterparts in the mainstream media mocked, marginalized or dismissed these claims as the ramblings of crackpots. But today, even journalists at corporate-owned newspapers and television stations are being forced to confront rogue elements within the White House and State Department.

In 2013, news surfaced that Obama organized a furtive network of secretive hit men that carried out the murders of individuals on his "kill list." Functioning in approximately 70 different countries, Obama's mercenaries were based out of the Joint Special Operations Command, or JSOC. Without trials and beyond the rule of law, anyone targeted by Obama, including their innocent family members, were subject to execution by drone strike.

On March 31, 2015 this writer contacted an alternative political researcher who requested that his name be withheld from publication. Speaking on this subject, the source began, "Off-the-books extra-government operations are the worst possible nightmare. American citizens are told that they enjoy a participatory government, but it's really only an illusion of freedom because secret operations are being run right under our noses. This government runs invisibly with no transparency or accountability. How soon will it be until there's a general acceptance of these secret governments?"

Branching out into other related topics, he conjectured, "Is ISIS actually the creation of intel agencies like the CIA, Mossad and MI5? If so, have they been instituted to incite permanent chaos and instability in the region so that it justifies more military action?"

He continued these thoughts. "ISIS could have been wiped out in a week or two. Look at Muammar Qadaffi, the leader of an actual government with an established army. It only took a few weeks to topple him in 2011. Yet Obama says it's going to take three-to-four years to wipe-out this ragtag band of fighters called ISIS. It's ridiculous."

No discussion of Libyan back channel paramilitary operations would be complete without focusing on then-Secretary of State Hillary Clinton. While employed at the State Department, Hillary not only maintained a private email server that allowed her to communicate beyond the parameters of federally-mandated oversights, she also formed her own personal intelligence agency that was commandeered by dirty tricks henchman Sidney Blumenthal and former CIA clandestine services officer Tyler Drumheller.

In addition to a vast weapons trafficking network extending from Benghazi to Syria, Clinton also weighed the possibility of placing contract military forces on the Libya-Tunisia border. Even more damning, Hillary learned weeks, even months, prior to the Benghazi consulate attack in which U.S. personnel were slain, that security levels could not withstand an onslaught by Islamic extremists. In this context, the Obama, Susan Rice, Jay Carney, and Clinton storyline about a spontaneous uprising caused by a YouTube video should be viewed as little more than outright deception.

It's not surprising that Mrs. Clinton subsequently wiped clean her private hard drive. Augmenting her off-the-books arrangements with sleaze-peddler Blumenthal and disinformation specialist Drumheller, a convincing amount of evidence points to Hillary financing all these expenditures with money laundered through her and husband Bill's Clinton Foundation. Unlike lawful State Department budgets which are congressionally approved, the Clinton Foundation faces no requirements in terms of donor lists, expense reports, or private slush funds used to pay off private mercenaries.

Sadly, too many details have yet to surface in the mainstream media. According to the previously mentioned source, "These shadow governments are invisible to the press and don't get attention like Blackwater did. The hard-core left isn't interested in covering this scandal because it's Obama's government that's doing it."

HILLARY CLINTON: NEOCON

As the Middle East simmers like a powder keg ready to explode, particularly nations such as Libya, Egypt, Iraq, Syria and Palestine, neocon strategists still loyal to Bush and Cheney's interventionist policies may now be ready to align with Hillary Clinton in 2016.

This sentiment was forwarded on July 5, 2014 by *The New York Times*'s Jacob Heilbrunn, who posited that diehard neocons like Richard Perle, Douglas Feith, Paul Wolfowitz and Paul Bremer may actually consider switching parties in the next presidential election if the GOP doesn't offer a candidate willing to advance their Israel-first agenda. Mrs. Clinton seems capable of fitting their bill perfectly, especially since she embraces big government liberal spending coupled with unrepentant militarism.

On July 9, 2014 this writer spoke with Michael McPherson, executive director of Veterans for Peace. McPherson began, "Hillary has a track record of being willing to take the U.S. into war. If this issue is your primary optic, it's difficult to accept her as the Democratic nominee."

McPherson expanded on this rationale. "After voting in support of the 2003 Iraqi war, it appears she hasn't learned a lesson and still advocates the same policies as 15 years ago."

Directing his attention to Clinton's advocacy of the U.S.-NATO led strike on Libya and sending arms to Syrian rebels, McPherson proposed, "Hillary was very hawkish as Secretary of State. Her stance on Libya and Syria are exactly the same track she'd follow as president. I'm very concerned that her past solutions are the same ones she'd follow in the future."

Likewise, on July 9, 2014 this writer interviewed Ollie Issa, national field organizer for the War Resisters League, who stated, "Hillary Clinton and Barack Obama claim to oppose war, yet they both supported vast troop increases in Afghanistan. They're both excellent examples of how elected officials haven't exerted influence on the Pentagon's military expenditures. To truly oppose war, Hillary and Obama wouldn't keep spending 45 cents of every dollar on the Defense Department."

Issa added, "Hillary represents that side of the Democratic Party which still wants to intervene militarily. When she OKed the strike on Libya, it was in the interest of weapons manufacturers who are constantly seeking new markets."

The same applies to Syria, as Issa surmised. "Clinton expresses a belief in U.S. foreign policy where we strike first and ask questions later. She's unwilling to admit that our policy in the Middle East has been disastrous. Rather, Hillary clings to a notion that the U.S. should be the world's policeman. This is a very old way of destructive thinking."

When the discussion turned to Clinton and former CIA Director Petraeus engineering a weapons-running program centered in Libya, Issa lamented, "Benghazi was a catastrophic and dismaying situation at a covert level. We'll never see any policy changes until the weapons industry and lobbyists quit profiting from the status quo."

Finally, on July 10, 2014 this writer reached out to Maria Santelli, director of the Center on Conscience and War. Bringing an element of stark realism to this situation, Santelli disclosed, "You don't get to be a potential candidate for president unless you play the game of war-profiteering. Unfortunately, Hillary Clinton wasn't courageous enough to stand up against the culture of war. The same applies to Obama, who's continued some of the Bush administration's worst policies on war. If someone's disillusioned about Obama now, it's because they had illusions about him before."

BEHIND THE NEOCON-AIPAC ALLIANCES

In 2008, Senator Hillary Clinton (D-N.Y.) was supposed to be enthroned as the Democrat's presidential nominee. However, one insurmountable obstacle stood in her way. Namely, progressives viewed Clinton as a pro-war candidate who intended to perpetuate the Bush administration's foreign policy. Hillary's support for the catastrophic Iraq war didn't help her standing among the liberal base either.

Eight years later, it appears that Clinton is slated yet again for another coronation in her bid to attain the White House. But, the question remains: has Hillary significantly changed her pro-war stance?

To get answers, on January 2, 2014 this writer contacted Robert Naiman, policy director for Just Foreign Policy, a non-partisan organization dedicated to reforming U.S. militarism.

Naiman told this writer, "In 2008, Hillary took a beating for her support of the Iraq war. But if we look at her track record as secretary of state under Barack Obama, she was an advocate for military intervention in Libya, and a cheerleader again for the same type of action against Syria. Hillary has been on the wrong side of the war issue ever since Iraq."

Specifically in terms of Libya, Naiman stated, "This U.S.-NATO invasion was a blatant violation of the War Powers Act and our Constitution. Plus, it wasn't a cakewalk like Hillary promised. It resulted in a breakdown of Libya's governmental order, which led to militia rule. Clearly, the tragedy that transpired in four deaths at our Benghazi consulate blew up in Hillary's face."

Connecting these incidents, Naiman explained, "A thread unites Iraq, Libya, Syria, and Iran. That's the AIPAC [American Israel Public Affairs Committee]-neocon influence. In 2008, Clinton was perceived as the AIPAC candidate. This is where her deepest allegiances lie."

Taking it a step further, Naiman continued, "As issues, AIPAC, war, and Wall Street are first cousins. The fact that Hillary is taking all this money from Wall Street is not unrelated to the people who want a war-like policy in the Middle East."

Indeed, on October 24 and 29, 2013 Goldman Sachs paid Clinton $400,000 for two speeches, one of which was specially hosted by CEO Lloyd Blankfein.

According to Naiman, this matter has unnerved certain factions. "Plenty of people in the Democratic Party aren't jazzed about Hillary being the 2016 nominee. The presumption is that it's all about AIPAC. As a New York senator, Clinton formed a deep relationship with the Israeli lobby's right wing. This bond indicates how she'd govern in the future and why Hillary vehemently opposes any deal with Iran."

Indeed, as a speaker at the 2008 AIPAC convention, Clinton pronounced, "I have a bedrock commitment to Israel's security." Also, on April 22, 2008 she told *Good Morning America* host Chris Cuomo, "I want the Iranians to know that if I'm president, we will attack Iran. In the next 10 years, during which [Iran] might foolishly consider launching an attack on Israel, we would be able to totally obliterate them."

In light of these harsh statements, on January 2, 2014 this writer also interviewed freelance writer Robert Barsocchini. On November 9, 2013 Barsocchini compiled an article entitled "Hillary Clinton's Pro-War and Imperialism Record in Bullet Points."

Barsocchini pointed out, "Hillary Clinton is part of a mindset that's a major threat to world peace. When examining the policies she supports, it's obvious from a moral perspective that human rights aren't a top priority. Instead, it's attacking countries that aren't in line strategically and politically with the U.S."

He further observed, "Clinton convinced the Obama administration to attack Libya without the permission of Congress. She was also completely in favor of overtly bombing the Syrians and covertly funding jihadists that opposed President Assad."

When questioned about Hillary's chances to become president in 2016, Barsocchini replied, "Hillary is a testament to the propaganda model."

CLINTON FOUNDATION JEOPARDIZES U.S. NATIONAL SECURITY?

U.S. national security has become dangerously compromised with news that the Russian state nuclear authority, Rosatom State Atomic Energy Corporation, now controls 20% of all American uranium deposits. Compounding matters, although a great deal of evidence indicates that then-Secretary of State Hillary Clinton peddled political influence in exchange for substantial contributions to her and husband Bill's foundation, many of the details may never emerge because Mrs. Clinton illegally erased documentation from the hard drive of her private email server.

To comprehend this situation's severity, on April 27, 2015 this writer contacted geologist Steve Mitchell, an expert on this subject due to his past research studies. From 1975-1981, Mitchell partook in the Natural Uranium Resources Evaluation (NURE) that was conducted by the Atomic Energy Commission (AEC). During the mid-1970s, Congress made the AEC responsible for determining what type of resources America had at its disposal.

Mitchell told this writer, "Under this $200 million program that took six years to complete, we evaluated all 48 continental states. The NURE concluded that there weren't nearly enough uranium resources in the U.S."

This point cannot be overemphasized, especially in terms of author Marin Katusa's book *The Colder War: How the Global Energy Trade Slipped from America's Grasp*. According to Katusa, the U.S. derives 20% of its electrical needs from nuclear power plants, yet it only produces one-fifth of the uranium required to meet these domestic needs. Worse, the majority of nuclear facilities only maintain uranium supplies which will last for 18-36 months.

Addressing these concerns, particularly how 20% of U.S. uranium is now controlled by a foreign entity, Mitchell continued, "Back in the 1970s, we never guessed that this type of deal would ever arise. I was dumbfounded when hearing the news. It blew me away that this situation could ever exist."

On the current-day significance of this predicament, Mitchell responded, "Let me reemphasize: the U.S. has no excess uranium. Allowing Russia to control any of our uranium resources is a potential problem because we don't have that much to begin with, at least not enough to feel secure. We need every bit of uranium that's on hand. It's absolutely terrible that this administration has allowed anyone outside the U.S. to control that amount of our resources. It's really bad news."

Every finger of blame should be directed at Hillary Clinton. When accepting her post as secretary of state, Hillary signed a document promising that her activities would be limited in regard to the Clinton Foundation. Moreover, she and Bill were required to publicly disclose every contributor, while all her governmental communications were supposed to transpire on State Department hardware. Hillary reneged on every one of these stipulations.

The greatest peril, though, lies in the fact that ARMZ, a Russian subsidiary of Rosatom that finalized the purchase of U.S. uranium mining rights, is forbidden by the Nuclear Regulatory Commission from exporting uranium without a license. Yet, in an April 23, 2015 *New York Times* article, Jo Becker and Mike McIntire stated that yellowcake—a concentrated powder-form byproduct derived from concentrated uranium—is routinely shipped into Canada via off-the-books shell companies. Any rogue nation that is capable of enriching uranium for military purposes, yet doesn't possess the proper fissile materials, desperately seeks yellowcake as part of the process needed to complete a weapons-grade nuclear bomb.

OBAMA AND HILLARY SELLING OUT U.S. TO UN

On February 7, 2012 former Clinton campaign manager Dick Morris dissected a host of international "sneaky treaties" that, he says, "Once signed and ratified, have the same status as constitutional law and cannot be altered or eclipsed by Congress or state legislatures. And, their provisions must be enforced by U.S. courts."

Quite possibly the most egregious of these would be U.S. membership in the International Criminal Court (ICC). This tribunal that has jurisdiction across the globe could prosecute elected U.S. leaders for entering into a war without UN approval. These "crimes of aggression"—even if approved by Congress under an official declaration of war—could still land the president or cabinet members in prison. Furthermore, the ICC's reach supersedes the rulings of any U.S. court, thereby posing a serious threat to constitutionally guaranteed trials by a jury of our peers.

A lesser-known aspect of this treaty involves, ironically, the use of America's military to wage "aggressions" against those deemed war criminals by the ICC. Already, Obama has buckled to this ruling body by sending armed forces into Africa to execute an arrest warrant for Joseph Kony, the leader of Uganda's Lord's Resistance Army.

Yet, rather than having Congress authorize the use of U.S. military members overseas, Obama bypassed them and opted to exert his executive power. He justified this decision as an "international obligation." One must ask: who is our president more obligated to: American citizens or the New World Order?

Another treaty, one advocating children's rights, would— at least superficially—protect youths from kidnapping, prostitution and human trafficking. However, if a 14-member panel determines that certain countries like the U.S. aren't providing enough funding for food, education or clothing to underdeveloped nations, the UN could, in essence, levy a tax on American citizens and then redistribute this foreign aid to those in the third world.

Not surprisingly, a leading proponent for the UN Convention on the Rights of the Child (UNCRC) is Hillary Clinton. In her book, *It Takes a Village*, she wrote, "The village must act in the place of parents. It accepts these responsibilities in all our names through the authority we vest in the government."

These 14-member overlords could also weigh in on what religious teachings, educational material, and social attitudes are acceptable. Interestingly, Hillary's views on child rearing dovetail with those of the UNCRC: "They [parents] have to be shown how to do it. They have to be, in a sense, re-parented to be able to be a good parent."

Hillary is so distrustful of traditional families that she further elaborated: "Decisions about motherhood and abortion, schooling, cosmetic surgery, treatment of venereal diseases, or employment, and others where the decision—or lack of one—will significantly reflect the child's future should not be made unilaterally by the parent."

If these social-engineering thoughts aren't horrifying enough, Clinton remarked at the University of Texas in 1993, "Let us be willing to remold society by redefining what it means to be a human being in the 20th century moving into the new millennium."

A third troublesome treaty is known as the Law of the Sea Treaty, or LOST. Today, America is the only nation not onboard. But, this situation may change if Obama sidesteps the Constitution yet again via executive order.

Although the complexities of this treaty are far too vast to elaborate on here, in a nutshell LOST will acquiesce to a UN council where U.S. companies can drill for oil and which technologies must become global property via a form of intellectual eminent domain. Worse yet, the UN could tax up to 50% of royalties from offshore drilling and redistribute these proceeds to poorer nations.

Lastly, the Outer Space Code of Conduct could seriously interfere with the U.S. implementing any type of anti-missile shield to protect itself. Using the feel-good premise of decreasing space debris, in actuality this treaty would jeopardize the U.S. military's ability to deploy platform-based weapons in space.

Superficially, some may support this idea. Yet, enforcement of such a notion is far-fetched at best, similar to speed limits on an interstate. Sure, laws are in place, but how many drivers adhere to them? When it comes to China and India's rapid development of their space programs and offensive weaponry, are Americans willing to forfeit their safety to the edicts of UN bureaucrats who already view us with such outright enmity?

WRITERS WARY OF GLOBALIST TREATIES

During a May 10, 2012 interview, Becky Fenger, a political columnist for Arizona's *Sonoran News*, voiced her concerns to this writer in regard to a rash of globalist treaties being negotiated by the current administration. "What are Hillary Clinton and Barack Obama thinking? I can't understand why they would willingly hand over power to the United Nations. How can you reason with these people when it seems like they've lost their minds?"

When questioned about the LOST and the International Criminal Court, Fenger replied, "Do you know how detrimental they are to our nation? We used to worry about communism and those who wanted to take over the U.S. But now we're surrendering our sovereignty to the UN, which is filled with lots of petty little dictators. America should get out of the UN since we pay the bulk of dues and always get voted against anyway."

According to Fenger, the dangers facing us are monumental. "These treaties become the equivalent of constitutional law, and it'll take 161 countries to release us from them. Worse, I'm not sure if Congress is even aware of what's going on, or if they understand how binding these treaties are."

A Hillary Clinton presidency will be a disaster for America.

She continued, "Look at the ICC. Aggression is described as going to war without UN approval, which includes Russia and China. What kind of mind thinks that succumbing to this is a good idea?"

Fenger next addressed one of Mrs. Clinton's favorite pet projects. "Hillary said it takes a village, not a parent, to raise children. Their goal is really to get these little minds and teach them from infancy ways to love global government dictatorship. But why should we relinquish parental control when it's been a guiding light throughout history? They want to disintegrate the family unit and replace it with government being the big daddy. It's unconscionable. Our personal liberties have always frightened them, so their goal is to take freedom out of the hands of every individual."

This writer also broached the subject of Obama's increasing use of executive orders. Fenger explained, "I used to think that a law couldn't pass if it was unconstitutional, but what about eminent domain and the Kelo decision? I've lost all faith in what used to be known as common sense and following the Constitution. Plus, Obama has proven that he doesn't give a damn about the Constitution."

Brandon Pierce, author of a fictionalized novel regarding the Bilderbergs entitled *Crisis Point*, agreed, telling this writer on May 11, 2012: "Barack Obama and Hillary Clinton are incrementally turning over our sovereignty to international bodies. They tell us we're supposed to be citizens of the world, but they don't have our best interests in mind."

In regard to the ICC, Pierce commented, "Americans could be tried in a world court even after they've been acquitted in the U.S. It has a direct effect on all of us when an international body can decide what happens to our leaders and citizens."

Scandals

HILLARY'S WAR ON CHILDREN

In 1975 attorney Hillary Clinton defended a 41-year-old child rapist who she knew was guilty. Hillary can be heard on recently unearthed tapes laughing about how, due to a technicality, she pleaded her client down to a two-month sentence of time already served after he got a 12-year-old girl drunk on whiskey and violated her in his car.

As she had done to innumerable women that her husband Bill had raped or preyed upon, Hillary viciously attacked this preteen victim as being "emotionally unstable" with a "tendency to seek out older men and engage in fantasizing." Hillary added, "I've been told by experts in child psychology that children in early adolescence exaggerate or romanticize sexual experiences."

This young girl—now aged 52 and speaking on condition of anonymity—responded to reporters about Hillary's tactics. "I realize the truth now, the heart of what she did to me. She's supposed to be for women? You call that being for women? I heard her on tape laughing. I don't think [Hillary's] a role model at all. If she had been, she would have helped me at the time . . . how many other lies has she told to get where she's at today? If she becomes president, will she tell the truth? No. She's going to tell lies . . . I'm a little scared of her. I'm worried she might try to hurt me."

Author Onan Coca summed it up best on June 21, 2014. "This is the woman Democrats want leading our nation? An unscrupulous liar who will do whatever it takes to get her way, even if it means terrorizing, demeaning and destroying a little girl who was an innocent victim to a violent and disgusting crime."

HILLARY, BILL & OBAMA'S ACORN CONNECTIONS

Similar to Cheney's Halliburton, Richard Nixon's Watergate, and the Clintons' Whitewater scandal, the Association of Community Organizations for Reform Now (ACORN) was a public relations albatross around Barack Hussein Obama's neck. The Feds investigated ACORN (now defunct) in a dozen states (voter fraud, accounting irregularities, etc.) and found confirmation that the founder's brother—Dale Rathke—embezzled nearly a million dollars.

By their own admission, ACORN covered-up Rathke's illegal activities to keep law enforcement off their heels, while in May 2009 *The New York Times* confessed to spiking a preelection story that connected ACORN to Democratic nominee Obama.

This article had been described as "game changing," and could have swayed the 2008 presidential outcome.

As more researchers pried into the shady dealings of ACORN, the Service Employees International Union, and the privately owned Citizens Consulting, Inc. (CCI), an interesting sidebar emerged. In 1970, Wade Rathke set up shop in Little Rock, Arkansas, home of the notorious Dixie Mafia, and one of the most corrupt venues imaginable. A long-time Rockefeller stronghold operated by kingmakers Witt and Jackson Stephens, this region also came under the heavy thumb of Senator J. William Fulbright (a globalist Rhodes Scholar), Don Tyson, Dan Lasater, the Clinton-created Arkansas Development Finance Authority (ADFA), the Bank of Credit and Commerce International (BCCI), and some extremely criminal activity at an airstrip in Mena.

Richard Odom summarizes the co-mingling of high finance and the underworld in his fine book, *Circle of Death*: "If Arkansas of the 1980s was something of a regional center for banking and small industry, it was also an international center for drug smuggling, gun-running, and money laundering operations."

Since Arkansas was at the nexus of this brewing firestorm, naturally Bill and Hillary Clinton gravitated toward the cesspool. The website "The Founding Bloggers" stated, "The connections between Wade Rathke (founder of ACORN) and the Clintons go way back. Don't forget: the "A" in ACORN originally stood for Arkansas [i.e., Arkansas Community Organization for Reform Now]."

While initially conceived as an offshoot of radical socialist George Wiley's National Welfare Reform Organization, ACORN quickly became more political by running and endorsing candidates in local elections. One of the first politicians they backed was a rising 32-year-old star named Bill Clinton, who became the youngest governor in the nation at the time. In a seminal book on Arkansas' favorite son entitled *On the Make*, journalist Meredith Oakley noted,

"ACORN gave early publicity and fundraising to Clinton due to his anti-utilities stance."

Needless to say, ACORN became intertwined with another charismatic young politician—Chicago's Barack Hussein Obama—who worked on one of their voter registration projects after receiving his law degree from Harvard. Although separated by time and locale, the links between these figures is uncanny (and most certainly not coincidental).

For starters, Hillary Clinton wrote her senior honors thesis at Wellesley College on Chicago's radical left-wing activist, Saul Alinsky. After forming ACORN in Little Rock, Wade Rathke enrolled his new recruits into a program at Syracuse University that was based on Alinsky's teachings. Rathke began his career as a "draft-resistance organizer for the Students for a Democratic Society (SDS)," whereas Bill Clinton used every conceivable power broker in Arkansas to facilitate his draft-dodging efforts.

Another famous SDS alumnus was William Ayers, himself a Saul Alinsky protégé and future Weather Underground Organization (WUO) terrorist. Of course, Obama kicked off his political career with a fundraiser at Ayers' home, while also working with him on the Woods Fund and Annenberg Challenge. Similarly, when the Clintons rendered their famous "PardonGate" before leaving the White House in 2001, they included two key members of the WUO.

While establishing itself in the early 1970s, ACORN's state chairwoman Dorothy Perkins labeled them "one of the biggest scams in Arkansas." An October 13, 2008 article on "The Founding Bloggers" clearly shows how this corruption led straight to the governor's mansion. "ACORN was an offshoot of the SDS/WUO, and they had done a lot of crooked stuff under (and for) Clinton back in Arkansas, and then in the general elections. They knew where Clinton's skeletons were buried, and so, he took care of them."

Bill and Hillary learned their lessons well, for in the 1980s they established the ADFA that took campaign financing to all-time lows. In essence, reminiscent of tactics used by BCCI, money laundered from Iran-Contra drugs-and-arms sales was funneled into the ADFA, which was supposedly started to assist low-income home buyers, small businesses, and to create jobs. But, akin to ACORN, a far different picture emerged. According to David Bresnahan, who wrote in his book entitled *Damage Control*, "In seven years, ADFA created 2,751 jobs. Each cost the taxpayer $13,202 to create—although the average salary was only $15,000."

There were other kickback scams, slush funds, and more importantly, millions of dollars directed into Bill Clinton's gubernatorial campaign coffers [not to mention his 1992 run for the Oval Office]. UK columnist Ambrose Evans-Pritchard called these funds "Bill Clinton's own political piggy bank." Also, it's now known that the ADFA worked hand-in-hand with Freddie Mac, Fannie Mae, and ACORN to secure home loans (many of which turned out badly) for Arkansas residents who couldn't afford them. This practice soon spread nationwide, creating a housing bubble that led to the subprime mortgage crisis.

The biggest variable right now is: why did Black Nationalist leader George Wiley (a predecessor to Obama's spiritual advisor, Reverend Jeremiah Wright) send Wade Rathke to Little Rock, Arkansas? It's this writer's contention that since Bill Clinton had long been selected to be the "chosen one," establishing ACORN in Arkansas was step one in mobilizing the

SDS-Weather Underground-black nationalist-extreme socialist contingent to amass power in this country.

Their subversive efforts, although largely unnoticed for many years, were horrifyingly effective when viewed in the following context. If the same man owned the New York Yankees and New York Mets and both teams played in the World Series, would it matter to him which one won? No, because both are under his umbrella. Well, the 1992 election pitted progressive globalist George H. W. Bush against progressive globalist Bill Clinton. "Slick Willie" served for eight years, and became, by his own account, "America's first black president." Then, after George W. Bush's disastrous reign, where one Skull and Bonesman ran against another Skull and Bonesman (John Kerry) in 2004, it was an almost foregone conclusion that a Democrat would win in 2008.

As a result, in the primaries, Little Rock-transplant Hillary Clinton and Chicago's Obama were both unabashed products of the above-mentioned political cabal. Obama got the nod, thus becoming America's second "black" ACORN-affiliated president.

HEALTHCARE HORROR SHOW

Ever since the mid-1990s when she strolled into the White House with her husband Bill, Hillary Clinton has been promoting government-controlled healthcare. Now that it's been implemented under the so-called Affordable Care Act, senior citizens should address this question: Are you ready to be euthanized? If you're an elderly American, especially one who doesn't walk in lockstep with the New World Order's plans to rid our planet of 'useless eaters,' you better prepare yourself for this possibility. Although most people aren't aware of it, PresidentObama's February 2009 stimulus bill contained the most draconian legislation this nation has ever seen. Hidden within this 1,000+ page document was health legislation which affects "every individual in the United States."

Obama touted this plan's urgent necessity, but what he really gave us is the first step toward European neo-socialism mixed with closed-market British rationing. Add a touch of Orwellian Big Brother collectivism, and it all eventually leads to gulag-style totalitarianism. Developed by Bilderberg and CFR member Tom Daschle in his book, *Critical: What We Can Do about the Health-Care Crisis*, we're now facing another big government takeover that has dire consequences if we ever get sick.

In simplest terms, a new bureaucracy has been formed, headed by a National Coordinator of Health Information Technology. Using a vast computer database, all medical treatments, in addition to other potential details (such as tax records, bank statements, police reports, and 'lifestyle choices'), are all tracked electronically. According to former New York lieutenant governor Betsy McCaughey's February 9, 2009 commentary on Bloomberg, "Ruin Your Health with the Obama Stimulus Plan," this 'Board' will "monitor treatments to make sure your doctor is doing what the federal government deems appropriate and cost effective."

Rather than abiding by the Hippocratic Oath in which the safe treatment of each patient takes precedence, this new agency will only proceed with a procedure if there is a distinct payoff for society. This paradigm shift in perspective is where Daschle's worldview becomes horrifying. In his book,

he praises Europeans who accept their "hopeless diagnoses."
In contrast, he feels Americans still expect too much from
the health care system and should instead simply "accept the
conditions that come with age."

Writing for "TownHall.com" on February 15, 2009,
Austin Hill begins, "Welcome to the era of Obama. You now
have a duty to die." Since doctors and hospitals will surrender their autonomy to a council of National Coordinators
who guide their decisions, Hill describes how "we now have
the beginnings of a governmental agency that eventually
will, by force of law, determine which persons will be eligi-
ble for health care, and what treatment they will receive."

If you're elderly, already sick with a preexisting condition,
or have few years left to work, then according to Daschle and
Obama's board, you have a "low return on investment," and
as such, it's your duty to die. If you refuse to follow these
edicts, then bureaucrats get to play God by deciding who
should perish by denying medical treatment.

Hill makes it crystal clear. "Once you have lived 'long
enough,' after you have consumed your 'fair share' of the earth's
resources, and when your combined age and health conditions
make it 'obvious' that further efforts to prolong your life just
simply 'aren't worth it,' you will then have a responsibility to
accept these consequences, and to accept that you'll just have
to get along without life-sustaining health care."

To ensure that these policies are followed, the bill refers
to doctors becoming "meaningful users" who must become
part of the system or face losing their license and/or government Medicare contracts. After studying this legislation,
journalist Byron Richards discovered on February 13, 2009
that the "quality and type of care will not be determined by

the doctor, but rather by a new system of cost containment implemented by the federal government."

As an incentive, the Board will give doctors bonuses (i.e., economic blackmail) if they comply with their mandates. Not only will they be encouraged to enter a patient's Electronic Health Records, but they must also practice the 'proper' kind of medicine. Frowned upon will be holistic medicines, vitamin therapy, alternative procedures, plus new remedies or technologies that drive up costs. Under this plan, the Board will issue life-and-death verdicts that politicians can safely stay distanced from. Or, as Tom Daschle recommends, senior citizens will have to accept conditions associated with old age because doctors will no longer be treating them.

To put the magnitude of this legislation into focus, Mc-Caughey states that our country's largest employer is the health care industry, comprising 17% of gross domestic product. Under Obama's plan, "The bill allocates more funding for this bureaucracy than for the Army, Navy, Marines, and Air Force combined." Fearing a repeat of Hillary Clinton's health care debacle in 1994, Daschle urged the president to sneak this legislation into another bill before any opposition arises, therefore bypassing Congress.

Once every American's records are entered into a labyrinthine electronic database, what comes next? Will our DNA samples soon be digitized, followed by computer microchips implanted into our bodies? We've just entered a brave new world that is terrifying in its reach, intrusiveness, and disregard for the sanctity of human life.

AFGHANISTAN DRUG TRADE KEEPS BOOMING

The tragic overdose death of acclaimed Academy Award-winning actor Philip Seymour Hoffman on February 2, 2014 brought renewed interest to the subject of cheap heroin on America's streets. Southwestern Pennsylvania suffered 22 overdoses in little over a week's time from tainted "smack," while dozens of users were hospitalized in Camden, N.J. due to highly potent "junk."

One of the big questions asked by naïve media talking heads is: what is the origin of this heroin? The answer is the same as it was in 2001-2002 following a CIA-led invasion of Afghanistan. Between 75-80% of the world's heroin is exported from Afghanistan, and in 2013 production levels hit record highs.

Since American forces have been entrenched in that country for a dozen years and have squandered over $700 billion to date, AFP has long been one of the few publications to openly address a highly taboo subject. Namely, elements within the CIA have been heavily involved with illegal narcotics trafficking since the Vietnam War and Iran-Contra.

On March 13, 2014 this writer contacted investigative historian Robert Morrow, whose research into the murder of CIA-sanctioned pilot Barry Seal is unparalleled. When asked about official criminality associated with Afghan's opium business, Morrow replied, "U.S. government involvement in the drug trade ebbs and flows depending on a particular administration's level of corruption. If a Bush or Clinton is in office, you better believe it's rip-roaring."

Morrow provided more insights. "Or, maybe their complicity is so institutionalized that presidents don't even control it. Intelligence agencies and the military do. The government has many faces. One Drug Enforcement Administration agent could be entirely honest while another is on the take from drug cartels and the government."

Delving into "deep state" specifics, Morrow stressed, "The people who ran all the drugs into America during the Iran-Contra era were George H. W. Bush, CIA Director William Casey, Oliver North, and both Clintons. Airports like the one in Mena, Arkansas that Bill and Hillary operated stretched all across the southern U.S. You need to remember that Barry Seal [who flew more cocaine into America than any pilot in history] was personal friends with Bill Clinton. He also spoke with H. W. Bush on a weekly basis."

Morrow next turned his attention to Clinton's partner-in-crime. "As Vice President, George H. W. Bush had all aspects of law enforcement answering to him. That way, legitimate police officers weren't arresting his CIA drug dealers."

Ending on a riveting note, Morrow said, "These topics aren't expressed in the mainstream media because it would be detrimental to the government's credibility. Nobody is supposed to know that certain elements running our country are drug dealers, murderers and thugs."

On March 13, 2014 this writer also spoke with Dean Henderson, author of *Big Oil & Their Bankers in the Persian Gulf: Four Horsemen, Eight Families & Their Global Intelligence, Narcotics & Terror Network.*

In terms of CIA links to the Afghani heroin trade, Henderson determined, "They've been running it from the get-go all the way back to when the *mujahideen* were formed. It's been the same game starting with Jimmy Carter's people through Reagan, the Bushes, Clinton, and now Obama."

Henderson provided more details. "After the Vietnam War, when heroin stopped coming out of the Golden Triangle (one of Asia's two main opium-producing areas), the CIA set-up bases near Afghanistan in the late 1970s. CIA asset Osama bin Laden helped train these men, and soon warlords were planting poppies. It doesn't take a rocket scientist to figure this out. Obama's advisors work for the same neocons as did Bush's. These same people do the dirty work."

IT'S TIME TO DEFUND PLANNED PARENTHOOD

On August 19, 2015 the Center for Medical Progress (CMP) released its seventh investigative videotape that chronicled an array of ghoulish abortion atrocities being carried out by clinicians and high-ranking officials at Planned Parenthood Federation of America (PPFA), an organization that receives approximately $500 million annually in U.S. taxpayer funds. In CMP's latest document, Holly O'Donnell, a former procurement technician at StemExpress, told how doctors used scissors to lacerate the face of a full-term aborted baby so that its intact brain could be removed. StemExpress, based in Placerville, Calif., buys body parts from PPFA and then dissects them for future sales and research.

Interestingly, contrary to PPFA's false narrative, senior contributor Amy Otto claimed in a July 22, 2015 *The Federalist* article that medical research does not even require fetal tissue. Otto wrote, "There is a plentiful source of non-controversial stem cells widely available without requiring a single abortion: the placenta. This organ is routinely discarded after the delivery of a healthy baby."

O'Donnell also described witnessing a baby with a still beating heart extracted from its mother's womb before being left to die. Others interviewed by CMP revealed how a toxic drug called Digoxin was injected into fetuses to kill them so that doctors could be shielded from partial-birth abortion lawsuits.

To obtain some expert analysis on this subject, on July 29, 2015 this writer reached out to Eric Scheidler, executive director of Pro-Life Action League. Schiedler began, "These videos show the cold-bloodedness of Planned Parenthood's staff and the callousness in which they talk about modifying a procedure to procure body parts that they can later sell."

This point is vital, as Scheidler noted, "Anyone that watches these videos can see that Planned Parenthood is unequivocally in the business of profiting from abortion. In fact, they're driven to profit from abortion, and there's a growing opinion among the populace that Planned Parenthood shouldn't be given taxpayer money."

In regard to the dehumanization process associated with mutilated fetuses and the trafficking of intact body parts, Scheidler demanded, "These videos depict how corrupting abortion is. Planned Parenthood presents themselves as safe, clean abortion providers, but we now know that they're closer to modern-day Josef Mengeles. At the very bottom of this corruption and exploitation we find someone like Dr. Kermit Gosnell."

As many AFP readers will recall, Gosnell was a Philadelphia abortionist convicted of first-degree murder in 2013 after killing three infants. He was also found guilty of involuntary manslaughter, as well as 21 felony counts for performing illegal late-term abortions. His graphic court case horrified the nation.

One presidential candidate speaking out against this barbarity is Dr. Ben Carson. On August 12, 2015 he touched the third-rail of abortion. "I know who [Planned Parenthood founder] Margaret Sanger is. I know that she believed in eugenics." Carson continued, "I think people should go back and read about Margaret Sanger who founded this place, a woman Hillary Clinton, by the way, says that she admires."

Carson's words are particularly insightful because both Clinton and Obama fully support the abortion of full-term babies all the way up until the 39th week of pregnancy. They've adopted this stance due to PPFA's huge influence over the Democratic Party via substantial campaign contributions.

SANCTUARY CITIES FACE BACKLASH

According to Barack Obama, his cabinet members, and all four Democratic presidential candidates—including Hillary Clinton and avowed socialist Bernie Sanders—the lives of illegal aliens are more important than the safety of law-abiding citizens living in this country. Indeed, Obama, Clinton and Sanders, not to mention Representative Nancy Pelosi (D-Calif.) and Senator Harry Reid (D-Nev.), all support the lawless idea of sanctuary cities.

The blatantly treasonous nature of these sanctuary cities came under increased scrutiny on July 1. 2015 when an illegal alien, 45-year-old Francisco Sanchez, randomly shot and murdered a 32-year-old white woman named Katie Steinle as she strolled along a San Francisco pier with her father. Sanchez, a seven-time convicted felon who had been deported back to Mexico on five previous occasions, stated that he chose San Francisco as his residence because of its status as a sanctuary city.

Not only has the Obama White House refused to denounce the existence of sanctuary cities, they took Arizona legislators to court in 2014 for trying to enforce federal immigration laws. Worse, when sanctuary cities refuse to obey a 1996 Supreme Court ruling that requires them to turn over criminal border-crossers to agencies like Immigration and Customs Enforcement, Obama turns a blind eye. According to Obama, these laws are "voluntary," thus explaining why so many Hispanic criminals are released back onto American streets.

Rather than highlighting the Obama administration's betrayal of our nation's laws, the mainstream media has instead castigated presidential candidate Donald Trump as a racist. But during his June 16 presidential announcement speech, Trump couldn't have been more correct. He boldly stated, "When Mexico sends its people, they're not sending their best. They're sending people that have lots of problems, and they're bringing those problems with us. They're bringing drugs. They're bringing crime. They're rapists. And some, I assume, are good people."

Not only have strong conservative voices such as Sheriff Joe Arpaio and Pat Buchanan lent their support to Trump, but a September 10, 2014 article in *Fusion* magazine confirmed the real estate mogul's assertions. They wrote, "A staggering 80% of Central American girls and women crossing Mexico *en route* to the United States are raped along the way, according to directors of migrant shelters interviewed by *Fusion*." Thousands of other similar crimes are perpetrated

118 | CROWNING CLINTON

by these criminal hordes.

To obtain some firsthand insights, on July 7, 2015 this writer interviewed C.J. Bryant of California's Nevada County Tea Party. Ms. Bryant began, "We grieve for the family of that young girl that was slain, but there are many more instances of illegals coming to this country and committing heinous crimes. Here's the question we keep asking: why do leaders like Barack Obama want them here? There's a bigger agenda at hand."

Following this line of thought, Bryant continued, "Never before in history has one president so disregarded the rule of law than Obama. He picks and chooses what laws he wants to follow. But immigration laws are not voluntary. Guards in San Francisco are told to release illegal aliens. They don't have a choice because they're ordered to do so."

Bryant then provided a specific example. "When citizens in Murrieta County were told by their city council that the U.S. government would be sending busloads of illegals to be housed at a Department of Homeland Security illegal immigrant facility, the locals went out on the streets and protested. So, busloads of La Raza members and the Brown Brigade were brought in to oppose them. In the Bay Area, the arrival of illegal aliens is not only permissible, it's encouraged. Then, after the same criminals are incarcerated, they're let out over and over again instead of being deported. The American people are being victimized."

Crowning Clinton
Why Hillary Shouldn't Be In the White House

AMERICAN FREE PRESS Corresponding Editor Victor Thorn picks up where he left off with his *Hillary (and Bill)* trilogy. In *Crowning Clinton,* Thorn provides groundbreaking information that mainstream media sources only caught up with months or even years afterward, if they had the courage to even touch it at all. Including more than 50 one-on-one interviews with experts, this collection taps into some of the nation's most astute political minds to present a preponderance of evidence as to why Hillary and Bill's return to 1600 Pennsylvania Avenue would be disastrous for America. For example, all in one place you'll find the *real* truth about the Benghazi scandal; Hillary's covering up of Bill's sexual assaults against innocent victims; the email scandal that has rocked her candidacy; her recent shady business dealings and money laundering; and much more. At a time when this nation's future hangs on a delicate thread, every argument must be made to prevent Bill and Hillary from inflicting any further damage on the nation. *Crowning Clinton* arrives at precisely the right time. This new, potent anthology is a must read for those who can't rely on other venues for their news. Softcover, 118 pages, $12 plus $4 S&H inside the U.S. from AMERICAN FREE PRESS, 16000 Trade Zone Avenue, Unit 406, Upper Marlboro, MD 20774. Call 1-888-699-6397 toll free to charge or visit www.AmericanFreePress.net

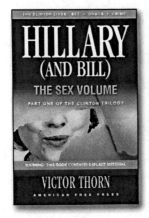
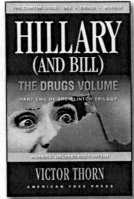
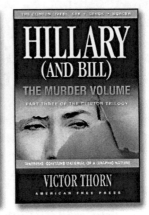

The Clinton Trilogy:
Sex, Drugs & Murder

HILLARY (And Bill): The SEX Volume

In *HILLARY (And Bill): The SEX Volume*—Part One of the Clinton Trilogy, Bill and Hillary's meteoric rise to success is chronicled. It's a carefully plotted path that eventually led them to the White House. But along the way, a series of compromises had to be made, including a prearranged marriage, clandestine assignments for the CIA, and Hillary's ultimate role as a "fixer" for her husband's many dalliances. Pulling no punches, investigative journalist Victor Thorn paints a compelling portrait of secrecy, deceit, violence, and betrayal that shatters the myth Mrs. Clinton has spent so many years trying to create. Softcover, 344 pages, $30

HILLARY (And Bill): The DRUGS Volume

In *HILLARY (And Bill): The DRUGS Volume*—Part Two of the Clinton Trilogy some of the most damning examples ever put into print of the U.S. government's crimes and corruption are exposed in glaring detail. Beginning with the Clinton family's long-standing ties to the notorious Dixie Mafia, this book illustrates how billions of dollars of cocaine, cash and weapons passed through Mena, Arkansas during the 1980s—with the the full knowledge of Bill and Hillary—to finance the illegal war in Nicaragua. (Tons of this CIA-imported coke helped fuel the cocaine epidemic of the 1980s) In short, Bill and Hillary's Arkansas became nothing less than a narco-republic, with little banks near Mena laundering more money than the big banks in New York City.

As this thoroughly sourced tale unfolds, the reader encounters a sordid cast of characters including George Bush the Elder (who ran the operation from the office of the VP in D.C.), Oliver North, Manuel Noriega, Webster Hubbell, Barry Seal, Dan Lasater and the Stephens Brothers. In addition, an undeniable amount of evidence proves that nearly every one of Bill Clinton's gubernatorial campaigns—including his 1992 presidential bid—was substantially financed with cocaine money. Softcover, 310 pages, $30.

HILLARY (And Bill): The MURDER Volume

In *HILLARY (and Bill): The MURDER Volume*—Part Three of the Clinton Trilogy, the "Clinton Body Count" is presented in all its gory detail. The most comprehensive study of its kind ever compiled, nearly 120 mysterious deaths are examined, beginning with the grisly murder of two teenage boys who "knew too much" about the illicit drug trafficking operation in Mena, Arkansas, Their murder was then covered-up by Clinton crony, Dr. Fahmy Malak.

After ascending to the presidency in 1992, more atrocities continued with the nationally televised massacre at Waco. Indisputable documents and testimony now prove that not only were FBI and Delta Forces responsible for starting the inferno and killing 80+ Branch Davidians (many of them innocent children), but that Hillary Clinton directed and commandeered the attack to destroy evidence of past government crimes—some related to the manufacture of weapons destined to be included in "Iran-Contra" gun running. Following this nightmare, the public was soon confronted with the "suicide" of Clinton insider Vince Foster. After thoroughly debunking the official version of events, Thorn reveals the identity of Foster's real murderer, as well as treasonous actions against the U.S. government and the involvement of a foreign intelligence agency. Other high profile cases are also investigated, such as the Oklahoma City bombing, which was in actuality an operation similar to what toppled the World Trade Center towers on Sept. 11, 2001; the murders of Jerry Parks, Danny Casolaro, and former CIA Director William Colby; plus Chinagate and the subsequent political assassination of Commerce Secretary Ron Brown. Despite the corporate media's dismissal of this subject, the Clinton Body Count (i.e., a veritable "Murder, Inc.") is very real and can no longer be discounted as mere coincidence. Softcover, 393 pages, $30.

GET THE COMPLETE TRILOGY FOR $60—reg. $90!

NEW SUBSCRIBER SPECIAL:

AMERICAN FREE PRESS
Special Subscription Deal

There is no other paper in America like AMERICAN FREE PRESS (AFP). Every week the hard-driving journalists at AMERICAN FREE PRESS dig for the truth—no matter where the facts may lead. AFP's reporting has been lauded by prominent personalities across the globe, while here at home the controlled media and global power elite try their best to make you believe what you are getting in mainstream publications and on the nightly news is "the whole truth." Nothing could be further from reality!

From the unanswered questions about 9-11, the free trade fiasco, the happenings in our corrupt Congress, uncontrolled immigration, to alternative health news and more, AFP tackles the toughest issues of the day with a candid and provocative reporting style that has earned us a host of devoted followers—and powerful enemies.

Isn't it time you started getting a fresh, honest approach to the news that can make or break the future of you and your family?

You'll find all that in AFP plus lots more. AFP is guaranteed to provide all the "sizzle" we promise or we will refund the unused portion of your subscription—no questions asked!

Special "FREE BOOKS" Offer!

Get a FREE copy of Victor Thorn's *Frontman: Barack Obama Exposed* ($20 retail) when you subscribe to AFP for ONE year (26 issues per year) for $49. Get TWO FREE BOOKS—*Frontman* PLUS *Hillary & Bill: The Murder Volume* ($30 retail)—when you subscribe to AFP for TWO years (52 issues) for $89. That's $50 in FREE gifts! Send payment to AFP, 16000 Trade Zone Avenue, Unit 406, Upper Marlboro, MD 20774. Call AFP toll free at 1-888-699-NEWS (6397) to charge. See other subscription offers at www.AmericanFreePress.net.

AMERICAN FREE PRESS ORDERING COUPON

Description/Title	Qty	Cost Ea.	Total
SUBTOTAL			
Add S&H on books*			
Send me a 1-year USA subscription to AFP for $49			
Send me a 2-year USA subscription to AFP for $89			
TOTAL			

*S&H ON BOOKS: Add $4 S&H on orders up to $25. Add $6 S&H on orders from $25.01 to $50. Add $8 S&H on orders from $50.01 to $75. Add $10 flat S&H on orders over $100. Note: Outside the U.S. email bookstore@AmericanFreePress.net for S&H. You may also subscribe to AFP or buy books at www.AmericanFreePress.net

PAYMENT OPTIONS: ❑ CHECK/MO ❑ VISA ❑ MC ❑ DISCOVER ❑ AMEX

Card # _____

Expiration Date _____ Signature _____

CC16

CUSTOMER INFORMATION:

NAME _____

ADDRESS _____

CITY/STATE/ZIP _____

RETURN WITH PAYMENT TO: AMERICAN FREE PRESS, 16000 Trade Zone Avenue, Unit 406, Upper Marlboro, MD 20774. Call 1-888-699-6397 toll free to charge.

CPSIA information can be obtained
at www.ICGtesting.com
Printed in the USA
FFOW05n0155310316

9 780988 199798